Lea Goldberg
Selected Poetry and Drama

Lea Goldberg

SELECTED POETRY AND DRAMA

POETRY SELECTED, TRANSLATED
AND WITH AN INTRODUCTION BY
Rachel Tzvia Back

DRAMA TRANSLATED BY
T.Carmi

The Toby Press

First Edition 2005

The Toby Press LLC
POB 8531, New Milford, CT 06776-8531, USA
& POB 2455, London W1A 5WY, England
www.tobypress.com

Translation of and Introduction to the Selected Poetry
Copyright © 2005 by Rachel Tzvia Back

Grateful acknowledgment is made to the editors of the
journals *Lyric* and *Poetry International Web,* and to Amia
Lieblich (author of *Learning About Lea*), for first publishing
some of these translations in earlier versions.

Translation of and Introduction to *Lady of the Castle*
© The Institute for the Translation of Hebrew Literature.

ISBN 1 59264 111 3, a *paperback* original

A cip catalogue record for this title is available from the British Library

Typeset in Garamond by Jerusalem Typesetting

Printed and bound in the United States by
Thomson-Shore Inc., Michigan

Contents

PART I

Acknowledgments, 3

Introduction, 11

Selected Poems, 25

Notes on the Poems, 205

Index of First Lines, 227

PART II

Introduction, 239

Drama: Lady of the Castle, 243

*

A Selected Bibliography of Books by Lea Goldberg, 315

About the Translators, 317

Part 1:
Selected Poems

Acknowledgments

In the years I have worked on this project, I have encountered
time and again a deep enthusiasm of many around me for the poetry
of Lea Goldberg. The names of these people are too many to list
here, but for their enthusiasm—translated into encouragement of
my work—I am deeply grateful.

I can, and am happy, to thank by name a few crucial people
whose help and support have been indispensable. I start with Avi Pan
and Gilad Alon from the wonderful Kiryat Tivon *Karon HaSfarim*
Bookstore who helped me find the volumes I needed, who always
remembered me when new editions of Goldberg's work came in,
and whose unflagging passion for books in general and Goldberg
specifically is inspiring. Many thanks to Shirley Kaufman and Lisa
Katz, for reading the poems, offering invaluable suggestions, and for
the ongoing support and poetic community they provide me. I owe
special and deep gratitude to Nita Schechet whose fine editorial pen
improved the introduction and notes immeasurably, to Anat Bratman
whose expert guidance in matters of Hebrew grammar was invaluable,
and to Yakov Azriel for his extraordinary elucidation of liturgical and

biblical phrases; I am aware of my good fortune to have friends such as these who are scholars in their own right and whose generous spirits lead them always to offer their help quickly and expansively. Special thanks also to Yiska Harani and Oded Gal who pointed me toward crucial Goldberg poems that I had overlooked. Many thanks to the editors at Toby Press for their useful input and for guiding this book to press. Finally, I am especially grateful to my father, Nathan Back, who responded comprehensively and most generously to my every query regarding Jewish sources.

I would like to acknowledge all previous translators of Goldberg's poetry—and of them, especially Robert Friend—for their devotion to Goldberg's work and their efforts at rendering it in English. I recognize with this acknowledgment that the translation of poetic texts is an ongoing and unfinished project, and that each new translator builds on the translators that came before. I am also deeply grateful to Tuvia Ruebner, whose work on Goldberg opened all doors.

To my lovely children—Daniel, Ariel and Talya—I owe thanks for their continuing interest in this book and for the ways they have allowed Goldberg's poetry to become a part of our family life; and to Yoni, my life-partner, I am grateful, always, for his enduring love, which makes all things possible.

This project was supported by a grant from the Ticktin-Back Family SEEN Fund; this grant provided me with the time to devote to this work, making the project possible. I am, as always, moved by and grateful for the great generosity and support of both my parents. These translations were also awarded a 2005 PEN Translation Fund Grant, for which I am very grateful.

Above all, I am indebted to Mark Braverman—poet, translator, cousin, dear friend—who accompanied me on every step of this journey. Mark's careful and tireless editing of the translations, and his fine musical ear attuned to the subtleties and resonances of Hebrew and to the rhythms of every lyrical phrase, made these translations immeasurably stronger than they would have been otherwise. In addition, his passion for the project and his readiness to ponder and debate with me every translation dilemma transformed the process into a joyous one. For the many ways he has enriched these translations, and my life, I am profoundly grateful.

Rachel Tzvia Back

Poems

Introduction *11*

About Myself *25*

Early Poems (1935–1942) 27

"I saw my God in the café" *29*

There Are Many Like Me *30*

To a Portrait of My Mother *31*

Pietà *32*

Childhood *33*

On Poverty 42

Prayers of Atonement *43*

"Your lit-up window lost to the blue nights" *45*

Stars of the Nile 46

The world is heavy on our eyelids 47

Ending 48

from **On the Flowering (1948)** 51

From Songs of the River *53*

   1. The River Sings to the Stone *53*

   2. The Tree Sings to the River *54*

   3. The Moon Sings to the River *55*

   4. The Girl Sings to the River *56*

   5. The Blade of Grass Sings to the River *57*

Small Poems *58*

On The Flowering (1–9) *60*

from Love Sonnets: *Ahava* (1, 3, 4, 7) *69*

The Lament of Odysseus *73*

From the Book of the Dead 74

"And will they ever come, days of forgiveness and grace" 76

Elul in the Galilee. *77*

In the Jerusalem Hills. *78*

from **Lightning in the Morning (1955)**. *83*

Lightning Toward Morning *85*

At Light's Border *86*

from Still Life. *88*

The Broken Vessel. *89*

April *Khamsin*. *90*

Trees. *91*

    1. Pine *91*

    2. Eucalyptus *92*

    3. The Castor-Oil Plant (Jonah's Tree) *93*

A Coat of Many Colors *94*

Small Poems. *95*

Poems of the Journey's End *96*

from The Love of Teresa De Meun (1, 3, 7, 8, 9, 10, 12) *98*

You Are Wondrous. *105*

A Night Psalm *107*

From the Songs of My Beloved Land. *108*

from **Last Words (1959)** **111**

From the Songs of Zion. *113*

On Nightmares' Trail. *115*

Last Words. *117*

Three Days. *119*

The Lovers on the Beach *121*

From My Mother's House *123*

Splinters of a Storm *125*

Illuminations *128*

from **With this Night (1964)** **131**

With this Night *133*

The Shortest Journey *134*

    1. Tel Aviv 1935. . . . . *134*

    2. Evening in the Café *135*

    3. A Rainy Autumn Night and a Clear Morning *136*

4. Then She Had *137*
5. I Walked Then *138*
6. The Shortest Journey *139*
Songs of a Foreign Woman *140*
A Nameless Journey *142*
A Look at a Bee *144*
From the Songs of Two Autumns. *146*
And a Third Autumn *148*
For One Who Does Not Believe *149*
Passed to Another World *151*
God Once Commanded Us *153*
Portrait of the Poet as an Old Man *154*
Far Away *156*
1. Even this Landscape *156*
2. And Of All the Dead *156*
3. It is Not the Sea *157*
4. Far Away *157*
5. Answer *158*
Toward Myself *159*

from **The Remains of Life (1978)** **161**
"A young poet suddenly falls silent" *163*
"And the poem I did not write". *164*
"In everything there is at least an eighth part". *165*
from Fragments *166*
On the Mount of Olives *167*
Jerusalem, Earthly and Heavenly *168*
"The clasp of sand and stone" *170*
"The day turned". *171*
"My entire life summed up in that one moment—" *172*
"There were questions" *173*
A Hike in the Hills. *174*
Small Poems. *176*
"The hills today are shadows of hills" *178*
"But it was a wondrous spring" *179*
Nightmare *180*

"Yes, I have more" *181*

"Of all your forgotten ones I" *182*

"I'll rise, I will rise" *183*

On the Dangers of Smoking *184*

The Remains of Life *185*

Sickness *187*

White Poplar Leaves *188*

Tomorrow I will die. *190*

And this will be the judgment. *191*

Uncollected Poems **193**

Those Who Knew Me Will Remember. *195*

My hands are pale *196*

Khamsin *197*

Ne'ilah / Closing. *198*

    1. The Sun Will Turn *198*

    2. Because the Day Fades *199*

    3. Open for Us a Gate *200*

    4. *Ne'ilah* *201*

Notes on the Poems. *203*

Introduction

1. Biography

"I walked with the boats / and I stood with the bridges"

Lea Goldberg was born in 1911 in Koenigsberg, East Prussia, and spent her early years in Kovno (now Kaunas), Lithuania. Her mother tongue was Russian, and her first poems, written when she was still a young girl, were in Russian. During World War 1, her family—like many other Jews—was exiled from Lithuania to Russia, where they wandered from place to place. The arduous and complicated journey back to Lithuania in 1917 was marked by a traumatic and fateful experience for the small Goldberg family: at one of the stops, Goldberg's father was pulled from the train, arrested and tortured.[1] As a result of this random violence, Goldberg's father suffered a debilitating

---

1 In her autobiographic novel entitled *And He is the Light*—written in third-person—Goldberg describes the event in the following words:

   The border police of the little country. Ignorant farmers in army uniforms, focused their gaze on father's yellow shoes. They said that these shoes were an obvious sign that he was a Bolshevik spy. Then they imprisoned him in an empty stable. And every day, for 10 days in a row, they took him out—as

mental illness, was consequently committed to a mental hospital and thereafter separated from the family. Goldberg's parents were officially divorced in 1931. Her father remained for Goldberg a shadowy figure of absence and threatening illness.

As a schoolgirl, Goldberg attended the Hebrew Gymnasium in Kovno and soon became fluent in Hebrew (in addition to Russian and German); it was at the Hebrew Gymnasium where she began writing Hebrew verse and where her first longings for "the return to Israel" found expression. At age seventeen she began her university studies in Kovno, and in 1930 she continued these studies at the Universities of Berlin and Bonn (where she earned a doctorate in Semitic studies in 1933). Throughout her schooling, Goldberg's teachers and professors recognized in the young scholar a voracious and insightful mind, and they predicted that she would have an impressive academic career. However, with even greater passion and commitment, Goldberg's energies were directed throughout this period to perfecting her Hebrew and to writing poems, which were published as early as 1933 in Hebrew journals such as *Petach*, *Ketuvim* and *Turim*. After a year of waiting for her immigration certificate from the British Mandatory Government of Palestine, Goldberg arrived in Tel Aviv in 1935 (together with the writer Shimon Gens as her fictitious husband); there, the published copy of her first book, *Smoke Rings,* awaited her as a "welcome" surprise, and Lea Goldberg quickly took her place among Israel's leading intellectuals and poets.

In her Tel Aviv years (1935–1952), Goldberg worked at a variety of jobs, including editor of the *Sifriyat Poalim* publishing house's children's books, literary consultant to the *Habima* theater and theater critic for the newspaper *Al HaMishmar*. In 1936, Goldberg facilitated the immigration to Israel of her mother, and the two women lived together until Goldberg's death in 1970. In 1952, Goldberg accepted an offer to become a lecturer in European literature at the Hebrew University of Jerusalem, and moved with her mother to the capital.

if they were about to execute him. This game went on for 10 days. And the man broke.... From there, there was nowhere to go but to the hospital. See *And He is the Light*, Tel Aviv: Sifriat Poalim, 1946, p. 25.

As her journals and letters attest, her academic career in Jerusalem was riddled with difficulties and obstacles, "intrigues…that the sane mind could not even invent."[2] Despite these difficulties, Goldberg was an extravagantly popular lecturer, with hundreds of students flocking to her lectures, which she delivered in a voice characterized as strange and smoke-filled. In 1963, she helped found the Department of Comparative Literature, which she chaired until her death.

Goldberg was a versatile and prolific writer, with published works that include poetry (ten collections), plays, literary criticism, verse and stories for children, novels, and volumes of translations of European classics into Hebrew (she translated from seven different languages).[3] Her books for children have made her a central figure in popular Israeli culture as generation after generation of children are raised on her now classic tales *My Friends from Arnon Street* (1943), *A Flat to Let* (1959), *The Absent-Minded Guy from Kefar Azar* (1968), and on the poetry collected in *What Do the Does Do?* (1944). She enjoyed similar sweeping popularity among adults, with many of her poems being set to music, establishing her work as central in both literary and popular Israeli culture.[4] Linked with Avraham Shlonsky and Natan Alterman as the second generation of poets in modern

2   From a 1956 letter, quoted in Tuvia Ruebner's monograph *Lea Goldberg* (Hebrew). Tel Aviv: Sifriyat Poalim, 1980, p. 220n. Note: all passages from Ruebner's book are my translations from the Hebrew.

3   The range of masterpieces translated by Goldberg into Hebrew include *War and Peace*, Petrarch's sonnets, the selected poetry of Nelly Sachs, stories by Chekhov, plays by Shakespeare, Molière, Ibsen and Strinberg, and many others.

4   Ruebner opens his monograph on Goldberg with the following anecdote:
On the sixth anniversary of the poet's death, we visited her grave, as we do every year. Her old mother remained standing by the grave. The cab-driver, who had driven her up to the Jerusalem cemetery, turned to her and said: 'Don't be sad. What is life? We live and are forgotten. But she is not forgotten. Every day we hear her songs are sung on the radio and the television, and her stories are told, even to the children (p. 9).
Yehuda Amichai offers the following remembrance of himself "…as a young soldier in the 1948 war carrying one of her little books, much torn and tattered, in my knapsack. […] Her poetry has meant much to me." This anecdote is taken from Amichai's "Foreword" to Robert Friend's translations of Goldberg in *Leah Goldberg: Selected Poems*. London: The Menard Press, 1976.

Hebrew letters, Goldberg's poetry remains little known outside the Hebrew-speaking world.

Lea Goldberg died of cancer in 1970, at the age of 59. She was awarded the Israel Prize posthumously that same year.

II. On the Poetry

"And these things came to me / and commanded: sing"

In a 1961 essay on the Russian poet Anna Akhmatova, Lea Goldberg describes the poetry of her European literary foremother as characterized by "a calculated, polished, wise and monastic simplicity that cannot be copied, [and] an exact observation of things…. It seems that what Akhmatova accomplishes in her love poems and in her short, lucid nature poems, no one [else] knows how to do…."[5] Without any qualifications, and with a similar tone of wonder, these same words may be aptly and accurately applied to Goldberg's own poetry, which—together with its sophistication, mastery of music and form, and abundant allusions to classical sources (biblical, mythological, European)—maintained a directness, lucidity and simplicity that have become the hallmark of her work. Eschewing the more ornate Hebrew of her literary predecessors and casting her poetic eye on the heart's isolated moments and the landscape's small elements (the bee, the broken branch, the pool of rainwater), Goldberg wrote poetry

Though her work has never fallen out of favor in Israeli culture, there has been renewed and strengthened attention to her work in the last few years, with evenings on national TV devoted to her poetry, a one-woman play about her life and work in the commercial theaters, and the issuing of a two-volume CD collection of her poems set to music, sung by the full spectrum of Israel's performing artists.

5   From Goldberg's "On Anna Ahkmatova" in *Mi-Dor U'Me'ever*, p. 265. Quoted by Ruth Kartun-Blum and Anat Weisman in "Foreword" and by Hamutal Bar-Yosef in "On the Flowering: Lea Goldberg and Symbolism" in *Encounters with a Poet: Essays on the Works of Lea Goldberg* (Hebrew). Tel Aviv: Sifriat Poalim, 2000, pp. 13–14 and 100. Note: all passages from this collection of essays are my translations from the Hebrew.

that was searingly honest, intimate and bare. Her poems of desire and unrequited love, of longing for landscapes—geographic and temporal—that are lost forever, of an immigrant's divided identity and sense of dislocation, of nature that is often unforgiving but always wondrous, were passionately embraced by a wide spectrum of readers who found in Goldberg a voice that spoke their hearts. As Robert Alter notes, she may not have been, "a commanding figure"—to no small degree denied that position by the patriarchal strictures of the literary circles of her day—but she was most certainly "a necessary one,"[6] and remains so today.

One need not look to Goldberg's words about others to find a description of her work. In *With this Night* (1964), the last poetry collection published in her lifetime, Lea Goldberg included a four-part poem entitled "About Myself" which may be read not only as an autobiographic portrait but also as her *ars poetica*. In the first section of this poem she writes:

> *My days are engraved in my poems*
> *like years in the rings of a tree*
> *like the years of my life in the furrows of my brow.*

> *I have no difficult words—*
> *valves of illusion.*
> *My images are*
> *transparent like windows in a church:*
> *through them*

---

6   Robert Alter, *Defenses of the Imagination: Jewish Writers and Modern Historical Crisis*. Philadelphia: Jewish Publication Society, 1977, p. 92. Using similar terms of necessity, Ariel Hirschfeld writes: "In the Hebrew culture of the 1940s and 50s, Goldberg's poetry was as necessary as air for breathing…. [Her] poetry was attentive to the violence within which Israeli civilization was draped: the severance from childhood homes, the decimation of Diaspora's Jewry, the animosity to nature embedded in Zionism, and she spoke to all this directly…. She experienced in her own life—in her childhood—the rupture of an entire generation, and the corrective took expression in [her] tragic and cathartic art." From "On the Cultural Role of Lea Goldberg" in *Encounters with a Poet: Essays on the Works of Lea Goldberg*, p. 150.

one can see
how the light of the sky shifts
and how my loves
fall
like dying birds.

Goldberg dismisses "difficult words" as unnatural in that they exercise a mechanical control over hallucinatory impressions ("valves of illusion"); she chooses for herself a mode of poetic communication that is "transparent like windows in a church". The external world, visible through the glass, is also framed and colored by the mediating medium of church windows—which are, in themselves, works of art. Thus, the seeming "transparency"—or simplicity—of her images and words is deceptive, for it hides a careful and considered aesthetic ordering of the world. The choice of a simile built around "church windows" foregrounds Goldberg's rootedness in European culture; indeed, even as she embraced Hebrew and incorporated into her work the astonishing range of Jewish and biblical allusions with which modern Hebrew is suffused,[7] Goldberg always remained also a European.

Through the glass of these metaphoric church windows, Goldberg directs the reader's mind's eye to two inter-related images: the shifting of the light sky and the loss of love. In a fashion characteristic of much of her work, the natural and the emotional—the external and internal landscapes—are inextricably intertwined. Thus, toward the section's end, a simple and direct image of the natural realm is quietly transformed into a stark and painful revelation of love's deaths—repeated and unrelenting.

In the second section of this same poem, Goldberg continues her self-portraiture, reflecting on place and poetic calling:

---

7   As Robert Alter beautifully articulates, a byproduct of the sheer longevity of Hebrew is that "…allusion is not an occasional or even frequent elective device but in many texts is the woof and warp of the poem…" See Alter's *Hebrew and Modernity*. Bloomington and Indiana: Indiana University Press, 1994, pp. 10–11.

Simply:
there was snow in one country
thorns in another
and a star from the airplane window
at night
above many countries.

And these things came to me
and commanded: sing.
And they said: we are words
and I surrendered and sang them.

While Hebrew was her chosen language[8] and Israel her chosen country, to the end of her life Goldberg remained intensely and emotionally linked to the landscapes of her European birthplace and childhood, and her poetry continued to express the two-fold sensibility, and longings, of an immigrant. This sensibility often resulted in a sense of being suspended (like the migrating bird, like the plane) between two places—in a sense, finally, of belonging nowhere at all (like "a star from the airplane window / at night / above many countries"). It is "the heartache of two homelands" ("Pine" p. 91), she writes—and it is a heartache that reverberates through her oeuvre, giving expression to the memories and yearnings of many in the young nation of immigrants. The implied inevitability of suspension between two landscapes described in the first stanza is brought to the fore in the second stanza in the absolute inevitability of the poems themselves.

---

8   Regarding Hebrew as her chosen language, Goldberg wrote the following in her autobiographic novel *And He is the Light*:
      ...she clearly remembered...one of her acquaintances in Berlin. He used to lean across the window of the Department of Semitics and finger a book whose letters were squared, and she could still hear his voice: "Choose a language as you would a ring. Yours is the right to choose a language as a wedding-ring and bless it: Behold thou art sanctified unto me!"
      Quoting the above passage, Dov Vardi notes that choosing Hebrew as one's language—for artistic creations and everyday use both—was "a central tenet of Jewish European youth of the 1920s." See Vardi's *New Hebrew Poetry*. Tel Aviv: Sefer Press, 1947, p. 46.

The "things" of Goldberg's world come to her in the shape of words and they command her to sing; she surrenders and sings. Inevitability and necessity are linked, as the poet perceives her poetic vocation in semi-religious terms: as a calling she has no choice but to answer. Indeed, despite the understated stance she adopts in her poetry, Goldberg believed that the role of poetry—all poetry in general, her own specifically—was nothing less than "to articulate the human condition, in its every detail and delicacy."[9]

III. On Form and Motifs

"The hills today are shadows of hills"

The seeming simplicity of Goldberg's work is accompanied always by a mastery of, and affinity for, formal verse. In the sonnet sequences, terzina tercets and other poems of similarly complex rhyming schemes collected in *On the Flowering* (1948) and *Lightning in the Morning* (1955), Goldberg explores the nature of love—which is, in her experience, most often forbidden, impossible and unrequited—and the negotiations of a human heart bound by life's inherent limits. The predetermined attributes of these formal poems demarcate the passion and desires expressed in their content. Through this tension between form and content, the poems manifest the confines of the human condition; the soar of image, rhythm and word *within* these confines manifests the triumph of the human spirit. Her earlier poems, collected in *Smoke Rings* (1935), *The Green-Eyed Stalk* (1940) and *From My Old Home* (1942), are also characterized by a propensity toward the formal, most often written in quatrains, with regular end-rhyme schemes. The regularity of Goldberg's rhymes, together with the simplicity of her language and the directness of the poems' emotional tenor, led some to foolishly dismiss her work as unsophisticated and undeveloped—an early fate suffered by her American predecessor

9   From a 1946 essay by Goldberg "On the Humor in the Works of Genssin"— quoted by Ruebner, p. 56.

Emily Dickinson. However, like Dickinson, Goldberg subtly subverts the very forms in which she is writing by unexpected rhymes, word connections (a particularly effective literary device in Hebrew because of the three-letter root form of most words), and startling imagery. The result is lyrical poetry that embraces the reader in familiar and pleasing sound patterns, even as it surprises and "makes new."

In Goldberg's later books *With this Night* (1964) and most markedly in the posthumously published *The Remains of Life* (1971), one encounters a departure from the earlier rigid rhyme schemes, meters and quatrains. In their place, Goldberg in this period favors shifting stanzaic arrangements and irregular line-length, determined—it seems—by an internal logic and breath. The later poems—stark, bold and unrelenting in their gaze—are more modernist than her earlier work, and in the sometimes truncated line and disrupted syntax, one can more forcefully sense the silence that is always encroaching on the borders of her poetry: "the one name of silence / grows and grows stronger" ("White Poplar Leaves" p. 188). However, the same commitment to the musical so characteristic of her earlier work remains in evidence, here accomplished through various non-metered sound patterns. In particular, Goldberg's poetry exhibits extensive usage of anaphora and epiphora—the repeating of words or phrases at the start, or at the end, of successive lines. These devices, rhetorical and musical in derivation and origin, contribute to the captivating, litany-like lyricism of her work.

The device of musical repetition may be seen as a formal twin to one of the central motifs favored by Goldberg: the motif of reflections—which are, literally, repetitions of visual images. Throughout her oeuvre, various types of reflections are described and examined, and Goldberg's poetry is replete with images of mirrors, rain-puddles, still bodies of water and windows, and with echoes as a type of sound-reflection. At all times, the world is itself as well as its reflected double, reversed and revised in the transformation into reflection. The focus on reflections may be read as Goldberg's insistence that every moment, every emotion, every small element on the horizon, deserves close study—reflected, so to speak, in the mind and heart—and that the poem itself is the poet's reflection of the world in word and image.

The abundance of mirrors in Goldberg's poetry also emphasizes the sometimes fairy-tale ambiance of her work, foregrounded in the early poems, where childhood landscapes are revisited and remembered. Finally, this motif accentuates the profound loneliness that permeates her work; time and again the speaking voice of the poems finds itself in an empty room, with no one for company but the reflection in the mirror.

The windows reflected in her work are sometimes mirroring mediums, sometimes the border between the inside and outside, a threshold one may or may not cross.[10] Goldberg's poetry returns repeatedly to places and times that straddle—or separate—two worlds: where river meets shore, sky meets earth, room meets yard, past meets present. Moments of transition (autumn and spring, dusk and dawn, waking and sleep, all moments of blossoming, all types of dying) are examined with unfailing directness, with an abiding acknowledgment of the great difficulty involved in all manners of passage. Thresholds also mark the borders between individuals—the figurative walls and barricades that disallow love and fulfillment, or the potential bridges across these dividing presences that bring love to fruition. Thus, the speaker of these poems (traditionally conflated with Goldberg herself) awakes on a doorstep, where "the watchman found me" ("Three Days" p. 119), where the possibilities intrinsic to places of change are finally fulfilled, or finally thwarted.

The doubling nature of the mirror or the window is one instance of an overriding duality apparent in Goldberg's work. The speaker in her poems is at all times aware of her own doubled identity—of calm external appearances wrestling with wild emotions, of

---

10 In his poem "In Memory of Lea Goldberg," poet and translator T. Carmi describes Goldberg herself as sitting "...for hours at her window / like a collector with a magnifying glass." In an earlier section of this same poem, Carmi also alludes to Goldberg's poem "A Look at a Bee," where the poetic gaze is directed at a bee crawling on the window, and in that position the bee is exposed and vulnerable (traditionally, this bee has been read as the poet's double). Thus, windows serve multiple and meaningful functions in Goldberg's work. For Carmi's poem, see *T. Carmi and Dan Pagis: Selected Poems*. Translated by Stephen Mitchell. Penguin Books, 1976.

"[a] mind frozen, [a] heart ablaze" ("The Love of Teresa De Meun" p. 98). Similarly, the poetry displays heightened attentiveness to the two cultures and the two landscapes of her life—to the "other" reality that goes on existing, though perhaps far from sight:

> *Snow fell*
> *and in a foreign land*
> *there was a war*
> *and they died in the snow*
> *(as they do here in the spring)*
> *in a foreign land.*
>
> "The Remains of Life" p. 186

As is evident from the stanza above, both landscapes are indelibly marked by violence and loss. Goldberg's poetry, however, touches on the violence only in understated fashion—a form of resistance, perhaps, to the violence itself and to the nationalistic or "mobilized" poetry of her day (see notes to "The Lament of Odysseus" p. 73 and "And will they ever come, days of forgiveness and grace" p. 76). Thus, a duality of negating forces expresses itself here too in the contrast between the poet's quiet and humble tone and the violent images being described, in the contrast between "the widow's dirge and the iron's clang / The orphan's cry and the crash of walls falling" ("The Lament of Odysseus"), and "all things…simple and alive" ("And will they ever come"). This contrast foregrounds Goldberg's own poetic commitment—through a century "stiffened by blood and terror"—to use her words "to remind humankind, every moment and every day, that the opportunity to return and be human is not lost."[11]

---

11 From her 1939 letter to the newspaper *HaShomer Ha'Tsair*, in the midst of the debate regarding the role of poetry in wartime. Quoted by Ruebner, p. 71.

iv. *On Translating Goldberg's Poetry*

"This is the hour of transition"

The art and craft of translation has been described as a process of choice and, as such, it is an exhilarating and disturbing process—exhilarating and disturbing because there is, as translator Gregory Rabassa writes, "precious little certainty about what we are doing."[12] Within this uncertainty, and with a strong conviction that Goldberg's own poetic choices were fully considered and conscious, I have chosen as my guiding principle to stay as close as possible to Goldberg's Hebrew originals. Thus, my translations reflect her idiosyncratic punctuation usage, her line-breaks, stanzaic arrangements, and her deviations from normative grammar (for example, a plural possessive pronoun with a singular noun). In places where it seems her choices were motivated primarily by the meter or rhyme of the line—which are already inevitably shifted in the translation process—I have allowed myself to deviate from the Hebrew.

As noted previously, many of Goldberg's poems are built around their end-rhyme scheme. In order not to force the English syntax into unnatural constructions and in order not to distort the content of her poems in an effort to reflect her end-rhymes, I have most often not recreated the end-rhyme pattern and have sought to capture the musical lyricism of her work through alternative patterns—primarily through alliteration, assonance, or rhymes within the lines. Goldberg's poems are fluid and flowing in sound—the English translations aspire to a similar effect.

The translations here represent approximately a quarter of the poems published in her three-volume *Collected Poems* (1986); this collection has Lea Goldberg's best known—and best loved—poems, together with many lesser known pieces that reflect the full range

12 From "No Two Snowflakes are Alike: Translation as Metaphor" in *The Craft of Translation*. Eds. John Biguenet and Rainer Schulte. Chicago: University of Chicago Press, 1989, p. 12.

of this astonishing poet. The poems represent every stage of her thirty-five-year poetic career, and strive to reflect also the changes in her prosody. At project's end, I am acutely aware of how much work remains to be done to fully reflect in English the vast beauty and versatility of Lea Goldberg's poetry—I trust this volume opens a door in that direction.

Rachel Tzvia Back
October, 2004

About Myself

I

My days are engraved in my poems
like years in the rings of a tree
like the years of my life in the furrows of my brow.

I have no difficult words—
valves of illusion.
My images are
transparent like windows in a church:
through them
one can see
how the light of the sky shifts
and how my loves
fall
like dying birds.

2

Simply:
there was snow in one country
thorns in another country
and a star from the airplane window
at night
above many countries.

And these things came to me
and commanded: sing.
And they said: we are words

and I surrendered and sang them.

And more: there was a long bridge
and a lamp across it
and the man who never came towards me
and I said: he never comes towards me.

3
It isn't necessary
not in the hours of humiliation
not in the hours of exaltation
not in the hours of despair.

The pact has since been sealed
between silence and me
and there are wordless paths
to buried dreams.

4
I never loved a city
because I was content in it
and I never hated a city
because I was sad in it.

Seven gates
to the beautiful city
and my memory leaves and enters it
with the sun and the storm.

Early Poems (1935–1942)

*

I saw my God in the café.
He was revealed in the cigarette smoke.
Depressed, sorry and slack
he hinted: "One can live still!"

He was nothing like the one I love:
nearer than he—and downcast,
like the transparent shadow of starlight
he did not fill the emptiness.

By the light of a pale and reddish dusk,
like one confessing his sins before death,
he knelt down to kiss man's feet
and to beg his forgiveness.

There Are Many Like Me

There are many like me: lonely and sad,
one writes poems, another sells her body,
a third convalesces in Davos,
and all of us drink thirstily from the bitter cup.

And all of us know:
        in the wilting rays of autumn-morning
the dream of a kiss becomes vapor and rises… not toward us.
And all of us see
        the world's warmth in the mothers' eyes,
        and no child is ours.
And all of us meet dark and cold wastelands
in the doorways of abandoned rooms.

And it's one and the same—
        to renounce body or spirit,
or to die slowly in the sanitariums of Davos—
so vast is this cup
so abundant its polluted drink,
and from the love of life and its loneliness
there is no escape.

To a Portrait of My Mother

Your portrait is so peaceful. You are other:
a bit proud and embarrassed at being—my mother.
Accompanying me with a yielding smile and a tear
and never asking: "Who?"

You never wondered, never raged, when I came
daily demanding: "Give me!"
With your own hands you brought me everything
only because I am—me.

And today you remember, more than I do,
my childhood sorrows, then you already understood:
when your grown daughter would come to you,
she would bring her grief that has grown too.

Yes. I'll come broken and not ask how you are.
I'll not cry in your arms, not whisper: "Mama!"
You'll know:
        He who left me was dearer to me than you are,
and you won't ask: "Who?"

Pietà

Once again distances…and the blood of falling leaves
on earth's wounds.
The skeletal arm of a tree stretches
toward the blind horizon.

Once again Heaven's sorrow weeps
over the corpse of autumn land.
Like a Madonna who is kneeling
over the body of the crucified.

Pietà—whispers the forest,
Pietà—autumn answers,
and silence opens a gate
toward peace of the Father's realm.

Only the wind sobs bitterly—
Judas weeping for his sin,
he kisses the feet of his beloved
begging the dead to forgive.

Childhood

1. Opening

Like stars that find their way to every window,
like day peeking into every opened eye,
like light,
fingers that touched the dream's last thread
and stirred joy, and fear faded
and song arose.

So simple,
so full and simple,
like a green meadow embracing the lost trail
and dew
     and daisy
        and dove.

2. The Beach

Because they were crimson the paths that wandered toward sunset
and the sand-flocks that slipped toward the sea,
because the gulls' wings reddened in the light of the sunset,
because all this was
here
      near
            now in the world—

Because only the peaks were festive and blue,
because God set down his heavy load,
all this was remembered and known.

But why did the little girl weep,
the girl in the white dress
alone on the sand?

3. The Yard

The ivy that climbed the dark walls of the hut,
and the gutter, and the barrel deep as a secret.
The fresh and sharp smell of summer rain.
The droplets on the poppy leaves
like melting pearls.

The shoulders loose and narrow and damp—
the little girl in a white dress—
the silent yard of enchanted paths.
The abundant joy
of first loneliness.

4. The Street

In streets such as these live the simplest folk—
gardeners. Their tanned hands—trunk and stalk and earth.
And in the pronounced vein on a hand

the pale blue of the sky and the pale blue of a glance.
They need no smile in their silent golden greeting.
Here they live, on her street, the simplest folk.

Her hair swirls before the day closing its eyes.
The grass breathes in the autumn.
The street—a lake of gold,
its silence—who will draw it forth?
And in the doorway stands the tall and grey gardener,
pears overflowing the basket.

5. The Mirror

The winds hide in the folds of the curtains
and the room is an island in the crescent moon's sea.
Inverted tales are reflected in the mirror—
the hunchback colt gallops through kingdoms,
a brother and sister walk in the woods,
the wolf and the hunter in the forest.

Seven kid goats wait for their mother,
a queen pricks her finger on a needle,
seven dwarfs celebrate their day,
and the island is a palace, the mirror a lake
where a ship with a high mast sails—
and a girl—content Cinderella—

little girl on a white ship
sets sail for another land.

6. Seven Kid Goats

Once upon a time in the high skies
there was a pre-star twilight.
Seven kid goats played all day
on the grave of the ravished wolf.

The largest goat is reflected in the mirror:
there is her wobbly home.
Seven kid goats toss balls
toward the round and white moon.

The little girl in the white dress
by herself—and seven kid goats.
Toward her from every corner moves
the living furniture.

7. Twilight
It was understood as pretend, all pretend, Perrault's tales,
"The Golden Library"—a red book, its margins gold.
Twilight enters the room. Day extinguishes its candle.
On the black piano shelf the chords are silent.

Awaiting those who will return:
they are returning from a funeral. Their mournful steps measured.
In a moment the door will rattle.
A hand shades the eyes of the girl who saw death
face to face.

8. The Forest

Pine needles. Their gold dark and warm.
Supine. Moss and trunks. A glance and a summit in blue.
The whisper of the forest in the wise and secret wind.
Oh such lofty trees!

Two drops on a spider web—two tears
stretched between branches in the agony of their innocence.
Perhaps a great tree has already grown
on the little brother's grave.

9. Garden

Cherry-resin—sweet and transparent,
to strip from the trunk, to take.
The heights at dawn and the garden in bloom
a white storm of flowering.

To climb a hill and shout out: "Brothers,
look at the luminance of the tree-tops!
Springs such as these! See how they are departing."
They are leaving for another's childhood.

On Poverty

1. Our Days

Our days are quiet like the child's slumber,
their secret known only by wind and sun.
We opened the door to clear-eyed poverty,
the poverty of bread, of blood and of song.

For the city is ours, its horizons too
and the psalm of your steps in the street.
Look, our hearts bud is bursting forth.
Very soon and the pain will take flight.

2. Prayer on Death

O let me die with my eyes wide open
on the threshold of your loving land,
a death poor and simple—like a sister
to the stalk, the tree, the stone.

I'll press my ear to the green meadow,
I'll hear: earth ringing—
the horses stamping their hooves, from afar, from afar,
and the small footstep of a child.

Prayers of Atonement

1

You came to me to open my eyes,
your body a glance a window a mirror,
you arrived like night embracing the owl
in darkness showing him all necessary things.

And I learned: a name for every eyelash and nail
for every strand of hair on bared flesh,
and the fragrance of childhood, of resin and pine,
was that night of the body's sweet scent.

If there were torments—then they voyaged toward you
my white sail on course toward your dark night.
Now allow me to leave, let me go, let me go
to kneel on the shores of forgiveness.

2

The month divined over chamomile leaves,
cast my torn-off days into the deep:
splendor and sin, sorrow and joy,
all—through the dream's unfolding.

So I bent over, tied your shoelaces,
accompanied you wordless to my doorpost.
And toward it, down all your pathways
my sadness, like a smile, bloomed.

And I knew all the vows of betrayal you vowed,
as I stored up for you days of peace.
And I bowed down my surrendering brow
when you returned, near and complete.

*

Your lit-up window lost to the blue nights
opens to my dream-prayer like the Holy Ark.
The rivers washed white the doorway of your house,
and the path to it is pure.

Because you crossed a spectrum of solitudes and your poem fell
                                                          silent
and you'll carry your wise heart into the blaze of your death—
please, let me live in this world
lonely like you.

Stars of the Nile

Carry your dream to the stars of the Nile,
rising from their bath, from the dark undefiled,
and their shore far away.
Shadow of a wing will flicker over their faces,
a wind stretched wide over the Nile stars,
and their shore far away.

Carry your dream to the black face of the Nile,
to the Nile's black radiance—
perhaps the star will remember your name,
and its shore far away.

*

The world is heavy on our eyelids.
Our heads are bent. Our weeping stilled.
The light at the edge of the sea is sealed.
The song is done.

Clouds pass by. The convoy is marching
in vaulted and shining silence.

We will be calm. We will be very calm.
The day fades. Our eyes are closed.

Ending

1

At night when I closed my eyes I saw a leaf.
Just a leaf—and I knew that it was good.
The rivers flow toward the sea and the sea is never filled,
and thus I knew that it was good.

Somewhere, on the graves of my dead, soft grass grows,
soft and green grass, fresh and wet.
And their blood flowed toward the sea and the sea is not filled,
my God, Creator of the Universe, you who make tree and leaf

grow,

my God, how can this be good?

2

I left and never returned.
I never wanted to return.
The past I never loved
became again my beloved past,
in a world I had left,
in snows, in wiltings, in blossoms.

The grey homeland
glows in memories' tears—
desolation of the distant city,
melancholic Sabbaths,
all that encircled me like fear
in the nights when I was a girl.
Loss that has no remedy
glows in memories' tears.

I left for another country,
the winds erased my footprints,
today with hidden shame
I long for my dead to come alive.
I left proud and rebellious
and who will hear my prayers?

3
I imagined that time had stood still,
that apple trees are standing as of old
in full bloom, or the autumn gardens
are still spreading their carpets of gold.

As though our world has not been shattered,
as though we've not seen all we've seen,
as though our house is still standing and our place
a white table set for feast.

All, all we once loved
rushes by in your moist eyes.
Don't look at me that way, it's pointless
to remember, what they call, forgotten memories.

The forgotten memories one cannot forget,
the losses one cannot escape—

4
Into this quiet the voice
of lost worlds will burst.
Day will lull me into drowsiness,
night will wake me from dreams.

The angel cries on my rooftop,
his tears drip down my window,
and my dead never rose.

No ram's horn calling out in the silence,
no shelter in the black gloom,
no escape from the weeping of angels.

The dead never rose.

from
On the Flowering (1948)

From Songs of the River

"A chorus of small voices"
Paul Verlaine

1. The River Sings to the Stone

I kissed the stone in the chill of her dream,
for I am the song and she is silence,
she is the riddle and I the riddler,
both of us fashioned from one eternity.

I kissed the stone, her lonely flesh.
She the vow of devotion and I the betrayer,
I am the fleeting and she what is,
she creation's secret, and I—their embodiment.

And I knew I touched a heart made mute:
I am the poet and she—the world.

2. The Tree Sings to the River

The one who bore my golden autumn,
swept away my blood with the falling leaves,
the one who sees my spring when it returns
each year in the seasons' turning,

my brother the river, lost forever,
new each day, and different and one,
my brother the current between two shores
flowing as I do between spring and fall.

For I am the bud and I am the fruit,
I am my future and I am my past,
I am the tree-trunk, barren, alone,
and you—my days and my song.

3. The Moon Sings to the River

I am the one on high,
I am the many in the deep.
My image, doubled image,
from the river looks back at me.

I am the truth on high,
I am the deceit of the deep.
My image in the lie of its destiny
from the river looks back at me.

Above—wrapped in silence,
in the deep I murmur and sing.
I, on high—am God;
in the river I am litanies.

4. The Girl Sings to the River

Where will the current carry my small face?
Why does it tear at my eyes?
My home is far off in the pine grove,
so sad the rustling of my pines.

The river seduced me with its joyful song,
called my name, singing out,
I came to it, following the sound,
I abandoned my mother's house.

And I am her only one, tender in years,
before me cruel waters rise—
where will the river carry my face?
Why does it tear at my eyes?

5. The Blade of Grass Sings to the River

Even to little ones like me,
one among ten thousand,
even to the children of the poor
on disenchantment's shores
the river murmurs, murmurs,
murmurs with love.

The caressing sun
touches it now and then,
my image is also reflected
in green waters,
in the river's depths
we are all deep.

My image that grows deeper
on its way to the sea
is devoured and disappears
at the edge of erasure.
And in the river's voice
with the river's hymns
the soul that has been silent
will speak the world's praise.

Small Poems

1. Night

A basket full of stars,
the fragrance of whispering grass,
deep,
deep in the dew,
my heart beats.

Now your footsteps come near.
A myriad of droplets tremble.
Deep,
deep in the dew,
my heart beats.

2. The Stars

The stars are very beautiful—
small bells around heaven's neck.
The stars are very beautiful
even tonight
the night of my anguish.

3. Tree

And it will bear so easily
its heavy bloom,
its splendor suits it.
With no boasting
it will wear spring's majesty.
And happiness is simple—
like duty.

4. At Dawn

Night passed me by
fierce as lightning,
a pale green star on the horizon
has already faded and is gone.

Again dawn comes
too heavy to bear,
again my child in his cradle
cries out in fear.

On The Flowering

for Avraham Ben Yitzhak

I

The overnight flowering of the castor-oil tree
warm and heavy crimson on the black of velvet leaves.
A row of trees leans into the barbed wire fence.

The sheep, weary to the bone, return
to their pens. The stormy blue has parachuted
a pearl-white cloud above their shoulder.

All this will be lost one day like light broken in the rapids.
All this will rise forever in the woods' scent and silence.
And in the soft and red sunset it is as though

the grass grows out of the quiet of my blood.

2

Old woman, sun-burnt and blue-eyed.
Her crown—grey-hair and suffering.
The pail silvers. From the barn-door

steamy breaths rise fertile and fresh.
Her milking hands—life's decree.
Thus quiet sailors grasp the cord.

The cows' submission. A cloudless morning.
A woman above the flowing white.
Profane light and antique secret entangled—

a sorceress upon her magic.

3

That death would rise up in his window
we knew: his even gaze
clear and cold as a grape-skin.

And through the skin a congested world
approached, flickering, yellow as a sated day,
cities, streams, also a multitude

of springs and a host of blossomings bursting forth.
And he walked burdened to the border's edge.
So a weary bull in the setting day

brings the harvest to the barn.

4
This firmament—straight and wide-edged.
Scorched, wingless and barren,
before your stoniness, Jerusalem!

Shadows like large birds caged within
your walls. The monasteries relinquish
the crucified to the heat of the rocks.

O how they rose, how they returned to the city
frightened sheep their backs stained red—
and the church fathers woke

to a prayer bleating from the clodded valley.

5

How the trains passed by! Silvered tracks
hummed long and longing in memory of homelands,
waters splashing, a sword's slash.

They touched night the lonely eyes
of passengers being carried off somewhere.
Shadows of branches, electric sparks and fear,

and pale fingers touching the dark,
and someone in a listening voice telling
of a son, a house facing the garden…

How trains sailed by, never to return.

6

A restless blossoming in the darkness of our garden.
As on a death-night he craves: To live!
Blood and luminous white settle in our eyes.

Terror and passion in the breathing of beasts.
Cool and light the proud crescent moon.
And the wakeful things are doubled images.

Night lives in the blood and in the scent,
in this death and in this desire.
And all the stars come down to bloom

in the stillness of your visionary hands.

7

To the solitary of the night: the storm has died.
The heart's open landscape sits under falling stars.
The quietude of union upon the forest.

You are one who wanders the paths.
You are upright before splendor and summit.
You are mute in the rustling of the leaves.

The constellations turn in a convoy
in the hiding-places of heaven, and among them
your loneliness treads, adorned

with virtue and compassion and grace.

8

How can we bring our dying heart
at dawn to the new day?
For then wine sparkles in the glass,

and the firmament straps on its bow,
then morning quickens in the hay
and dusk's cheek caresses the river's brow.

And only we, fear-struck,
dream-bereft, witnesses of the blaze,
carry our blossoming land

like a mourning wreath toward the grave.

9
One abandoned star in the wild dark,
and the sound of the sea. Waves rise—despair.
A black desert facing breakers and wind.

Gloom leans forward—lump to lump.
Heaven's night will graze the sea's night,
and only one star, abandoned star,

soft, green bud of the sky,
spark of blossoms, herald of dreams:
perhaps somewhere higher than all heights—

the eternal spring has bloomed, has bloomed.

from Love Sonnets: *Ahava**

I
You were for me blessed earth
on which my step wouldn't falter,
like land which nourishes unknowingly
the modest stalk, the rich blossomings.

You were for me reward and forgiveness
for the wildness of my grief-ravaged ways,
As the river to the forest's edge
I fastened myself, knelt in your shade.

And your fine and humble gaze
showered on me the radiance of living things,
like a tiny dew-drop on the branch—

within it, clear unclouded distances
and the heights of a winged heaven.

---

* The letters of the word *Ahava* [the Hebrew word for love] equal the number 13;
thus, the *Ahava* sonnets are 13 lines long.

3
Today I remember your boyhood
as though I saw it with my own eyes,
as though it continues in me still,
like a tree's trunk, my love—its summit.

Only your mother's image withdraws and is gone
in her black dress of rustling silk,
lost in mists, becoming blurred—
sorrow's soft mystery unsolved.

But it's her voice I sometimes hear
within my own: with a desperate plea,
with "sweet dreams", with surrendering worry.

I hear your mother's voice and guess
at all her love, shy and abashed.

4

An aged moon adorned with the heat-wave's halo,
and a dark sea carrying the burden of silence,
somewhere, on a far-off and fading ship
already the lamps have been lit.

The evening is heavy. Don't go. Wait.
Look: our ship has sailed
and we on the shore with our sorrow
cling like babies to the rails.

Our hearts have sailed like a driven leaf,
gone with the waves on its wanderings,
there it shines on the curling crests.

And we are sad. How sweet is sorrow
when we can be sad together.

7

A sudden shower at the edge of April.
Our city's evening is golden-brown.
With pale light the city lamps try
to shine on us through slanting rain.

This heart's joy will not be restrained.
Don't hurry, don't hurry to leave!
Let us remember this blessed hour—
this surprising rain in late spring.

How good to be alone together in the street.
The flickering chain of lights
so lovely in the blowing wind.

Today I am soft and in love,
I am with you today—and it is good, it is good...

The Lament of Odysseus

Sated with wandering, old Odysseus descended to the Underworld
to pay his respects to friends killed by the sword.
The shadows of slain comrades greeted him at the gate,
their weeping and death cries resounding in his ears—
How the mighty have fallen!

Men and their steed fell in the killing fields.
The blood of beast and man—black rivers flowing.
Sound of the widow's dirge and the iron's clang.
The orphans' cry and the crash of walls falling.
Woe to eyes blind in the face of death,
woe to mute lips—"Give me water!"
How the mighty have fallen!

Above the stench and rotting, the vulture flies.
Among the dead, the living are lonely sevenfold.
I have come to this hell to ask for your pardon,
for the snare is broken, blasted open, and we have fled.
The death of a comrade is Cain's mark on my forehead.
My far-away life is Cain's mark on my forehead.
Your death cries resound in my ears.
How the mighty have fallen!

From the Book of the Dead

I
And beyond the land of the living
a steep path
rose
through the ravines,
through the sparse moss,
through the salt-licks
in a dry wind
until the wall's border.

There I stumbled and fell
beside the wall.
And there was no one to hear the confession,
no punishment and no reward,
no raven and no vulture,
no hyena
to crave the rotting flesh.

And the silence did not want my prayer.
On a transparent night,
in the high heavens
no star was lit.

from On the Flowering (1948)

2
I waited seven days for a tear to fall
in memory of what was.
But you did not give me the rites of last-tear
and so I will not rise from the dead.

I waited seven nights for the dream you would dream
to bring back my sorrowful self.
And even on the seventh night you did not dream of me,
so I will not rise from the dead.

In the seven days and seven nights
since my death you have not called out my name.
Why then should I rise from the dead,
for whom?

*

And will they ever come, days of forgiveness and grace,
when you'll walk in the fields, simple wanderer,
and your bare soles will be caressed by the clover,
or the wheat-stubble will sting your feet, and its sting will be
                                                        sweet?

Or the rainfall will catch you, its downpour pounding
on your shoulders, your breast, your neck, your head.
And you'll walk in the wet fields, quiet widening within
like light on the cloud's rim.

And you'll breathe in the scent of the furrow, full and calm,
and you'll see the sun in the rain-pool's golden mirror,
and all things are simple and alive, you may touch them,
and you are allowed, you are allowed to love.

You'll walk in the field. Alone, unscorched by the blaze
of the fires, along roads stiffened with blood and terror.
And true to your heart you'll be again humble and softened,
as one of the grass, as one of humankind.

Elul in the Galilee

1

A hundred silences and not one tear.
Mountains without utterance.
We walked weary through the thistles
the wind facing southward.

At the crossroads an olive tree, old and contented,
lonely as you are from summit to root,
abandoned its ancient head to an eternal wind.
We walked surrendering among the thistles
and it was evening.

2

Remember me kindly in such an autumn
among the burnt mountains,
when snakes emerge from their hiding-places
slithering mutely and begging for rain,
when the tree is weary of bearing its fruit,
and all who are tired are just like it.

.

In the Jerusalem Hills

I

I lie like a stone among these hills,
in yellow grass, wind-blasted and scorched by summer,
indifferent and silent.
A pale sky touches the boulders.
From where has this yellow-winged butterfly come?
A stone among stones—I do not know
how ancient my life is
or who will yet come
and kick me with his foot
to send me rolling down the slope.

Perhaps this is beauty frozen forever.
Perhaps this is
eternity, slowly walking by.
Perhaps this is
the dream of death
and of the one love.

I lie like a stone among these hills,
between thorns and thistles,
across from the road slipping toward town.
A wind that blesses all things will come
to caress the pine treetops
and the mute stones.

2
All things which are
outside love
come to me now—
this landscape and its old-age wisdom
which asks to live
one more year, one more year,
one more generation, another two, another three,
one more eternity.

To grow thorns endlessly,
to rock dead stones
like babies in their cradles before sleep.
To silence ancient memories,
one more, another two, another three...

O, how great is the hunger for life
of those who lean toward death.
How terrible the desire
and how empty—
to be, to be
one more year, one more year,
one more generation, another two, another three,
one more eternity.

3

How could a blithe bird stray
into these hills?
A love song in her throat,
her small heart quivering with joy.
Soon there will be chicks in her nest,
the beating of her wings a love hymn.

When suddenly from the blue heights
a wasteland beneath her
is revealed
a wasteland of stones and stonings.

Save her,
save her,
lest her eyes see
the corpse of every love,
the grave of every joy.

In her blue
heights
singing a solitary love song
she is suspended
and does not grasp
this death
before her.

4
How can one lone bird
carry the entire sky
on fragile
wings
above the desolation?
The sky is vast and blue,
resting on her wings
upheld by the power of her song.

So my heart carried its love,
which was vast and blue
higher than all heights,
above the desolation
and the debris of ruin
and the depths of despair.

Until my heart's song was silent
its strength spent and it
became like a stone
and fell.

My wounded love, mute love—
how can one lone bird
carry the entire sky!

from
Lightning in the Morning
(1955)

Lightning Toward Morning

Lightning and dawn. Light struck light.
The fencing of two knights.
Arms drawn from the sheath of dark
and thunder trumpeting from afar.

Black clouds and a ravaged horizon—
the skies with no mercy, no compassion.
And again dawn and lightning duel
to the water torrents' whistling tune.

Thus day is born. And it begins to live
in a warrior's light, with a two-edged sword.

At Light's Border

I

Here heavy birds alight to rest
on trees dark in the day's decline,
and in reaped fields the wind wanders
toward the firmament's red trail.

A gust of salt air from across the sea,
a crescent moon painting itself on the sky,
a flickering white, cautious, unsure
it is all vacillation between day and night.

This is the hour of transition wherein we stand mute
at light's border—
where will our hearts turn?
Will we return, my brother,
will we cross over?

2

All the riddles time has posed
skies like these awaken anew,
the innocent will tell their dreams
and the clever their answers conceal.

And again our hearts will bathe in blood
as empty regrets guard every step,
and again you unknowingly ask
all the riddles time has kept.

My brother, my brother, how can we stand mute
at light's border—
what path is before us?
Will we return, my brother,
will we cross over?

from Still Life

The Mirror

Deep within the mirror it lives—
the rest of my face, of my books,
deep within the polished space,
in a light of different radiance
it takes on new meaning.
Is this the way it lives in my songs?

Reversed within the mirror it lives—
the rest of my face, of my books.
The letters on every page
in the plain meaning of each title
become coded writing.
A truth known and different,
the truth of mirrors and of those who sing.

The Broken Vessel

1

They don't want to remember the truth
which was cold and negating.
They paint pink the face of the dead
and wrap him in white lies.

Only I, with a fearful memory,
press trembling lips to a cold hand
and before knowledge that will not forgive
as I extend my neck to the yoke, I kneel.

2

The cruel dawn
the broken vessel—
death's image on the empty terrain.

Red is the mountain.
And the lark who sings
upon his high places is slain.

April *Khamsin*

Yes, I know this is a peerless day
when nothing happened, nothing changed
no omen or sign, evil or good,
to mark it as different in any way.

Only the sun has the scent of jasmine,
only the stone has the sound of a beating heart,
only evening has the color of an orange,
only the sand has a kissing mouth.

How will I remember it, anonymous and plain,
how will I preserve its unexpected grace,
how will I believe there was one day
when every scent and stir was a part of me?

For every tree was a fluttering sail,
and silence had a young girl's eyes,
and tears the smell of blossomings,
and the name of the city was like my love's.

Trees

1. Pine

Here I cannot hear the voice of the cuckoo.
Here the tree will never wear a cape of snow.
But it is here in the shade of these pines
my entire childhood comes alive.

The chime of the needles: Once upon a time—
I called the snow-space homeland,
and the green ice that enchains the stream,
and the poem's tongue in a foreign land.

Perhaps only migrating birds know—
suspended as they are between earth and sky—
this heartache of two homelands.

With you I was transplanted twice,
with you, pine trees, I grew,
my roots in two different lands.

2. Eucalyptus

And if ever I am asked to say
how my spirit was redeemed,
I'll stay silent. My Savior, my Rock,
you will forgive—I cannot.

I cannot take in vain the name
of the Hell which was
my love. Leave me be now, leave
me as I am, wherever I am.

Let me be as mute as the tree
which was felled and again grew branches:
all the birds in its fallen summit
speak Heaven's praises, without it.

And it, alone and singular
remembers the blade of the honed axe,
and it, alone and mute
bears the full weight of perfect joy.

3. The Castor-Oil Plant (Jonah's Tree)

I saw a body stripped bare
stretched out on blood-drenched earth,
and two stars up high,
only two in all of heaven, both blind.

When suddenly a flawless tree bloomed
and with every leaf it sheltered the body
from heaven's blindness.

Night passes. Dawn will break
and a brutal sun will send out a legion
of annihilating rays, until every

night creature dies. Oh Lord, spare me,
Jonah's tree and all I see.

A Coat of Many Colors

We are dreamers. Don't fool
yourself, that you are sober and severe.
The brutal spring will rise in your throat,
wash away your visions, convert you.

And you'll wake and see the dream slain,
and you'll seek refuge in quiet and cold.
But morning will strike you with light and dew
and hang tears on your lashes.

Your lucid world will shatter to pieces
when it touches the heart of the hardened world:
because your father dressed you in a coat of colors,
on the altar your brothers will sacrifice you.

Small Poems

1. Like the light ray

Like the light ray that passes through
the crystal cup and piercing its heart
awakens in it the play of colors
and the dance of sparks that slept,
so too the memory of your glance
from long ago passed through me.
Did you hear?—Tonight I laughed.

2. In the Twilight of My Days

The curls on my head silver in the moonlight.
Baby birds sleep in the tree-branches across from me.
I tear open my window and cry out: Dove, come to me!
But night sends me wise owls instead.

3. Time

How the passing of Time tries me,
its double reckoning my duty and my right:
Every day it constructs and ruins me
completing thus my life and my death.

Poems of the Journey's End

I

The path is so lovely—said the boy.
The path is so hard—said the lad.
The path is so long—said the man.
The grandfather sat on the side of the path to rest.

Sunset paints his grey head gold and red,
the grass glows at his feet in the evening dew,
above him the day's last bird sings:
—Will you remember how lovely, how hard, how long was the
                                                    path?

2

You said: Day chases day and night—night.
In your heart you said: Now the time has come.
You see evenings and mornings visit your window,
and you say: There is nothing new under the sun.

Now, with the days, you have whitened and aged
your days numbered and tenfold dearer,
and you know: Every day is the last under the sun,
and you know: Every day is new under the sun.

3
Teach me, my God, to bless and pray
over the withered leaf's secret, the ready fruit's grace,
over this freedom: to see, to feel, to breath,
to know, to hope, to fail.

Teach my lips blessing and song of praise
when your days are renewed morning and night,
lest my day be today like all the yesterdays,
lest my day be for me an unthinking haze.

from The Love of Teresa De Meun

[*Teresa de Meun was a late 16th century French noblewoman. When she was about 40 years of age, she fell in love with the young Italian tutor of her children, and wrote 41 sonnets to him. When the young Italian left her house, she burned the poems and entered a nunnery. Only the memory of her poems remains—a legend told by generations to come.*]

I

This unrelenting curse with which I am cursed,
the innocent call it Love—
oh, if you knew how I've sunk, how low,
how contemptible in its suffering is my soul.

Strands of old age already silver my curls,
and I've nurtured the wisdom of years,
how then can I accept how foolish I am
all for a single unanswered glance.

Oh, pity me in my autumn day which was
lucid and exalted in the afternoon light.
Oh, take pity on my age, its wisdom too.

Like a doe my night's peace flees.
And this the disgrace: if I but close my eyes
my rebellious body cries out - You!

3
And were you to banish me to the desert
abandon me to loneliness and sorrow
to death, to hunger, to wild-beasts,
as Abraham banished his bondmaid Hagar,

if my heart's blood spilled forth before your eyes,
if you abused me like a concubine,
still my spirits would not rise up and rebel,
nor would my cry would be bitter and dry.

But I am for you exalted, untouchable,
a noble lady whose name
you dare not take in vain.

A fortified wall. The way is blocked.
The fear of disgrace restrains every step
and my fists pound on the barricade.

7

Long hours, little moments too
we shared, my quiet companion,
another day gone and again my soul wonders
what has slipped away in helpless silence.

What will testify to the years gone by,
to the saturated day, long and high—
is it just a crease on the smooth face,
a silver strand finding its place amid curls?

Truly, I haven't the spirit to stop the sun
in Givon, for me the moon
will not halt in Ayalon.

Hurried-in-haste my days passed by,
but every hour blessed with light
still flows in my blood—forever mine.

8

The strands of rain like violin strings
dangle on my window. My friend, light the fire
in the hearth. We will sit between rings
of light, and reflections will play around us.

The gray backdrop of a rainy day
suits you. Your youth so lovely
in the doubled light of autumn and flame—
my mind frozen, my heart ablaze.

How sweet is this deception:
my passion hidden and your innocence
entranced by my maternal glow.

And not a suspicion darkens your brow,
that here, beside the dancing coals,
I stole an hour of love.

9

From my window and from yours
the same garden, same view,
and for one perfect day I may love
all that your eyes have caressed.

Outside my window and outside yours
the same night songbird sings,
and when your heart quivers in its dreams
I awake and listen to him too.

The ancient pine whose every needle
carries your glance like pure dew,
will greet me with morning—

we loved so many things together
but the light never shone in your small window
when my loneliness touched yours.

10

Oh, how beautiful was the city that day
in her luminous circle of hills,
how her graceful old age glowed
in the bright light of your youthful eyes.

How the tops of the towers softened
in the splendor of your wise smile.
The alleyways rushed toward you
like a herd of devoted doe.

We stood enchanted at the threshold
rooted in the stillness of the space
like a pair of contented trees—

a blossoming almond tree beside an aged olive.
How the boulders budded in the dew,
how the stones of the hills bloomed!

12

What will remain? Words, words like the ash
of this fire which consumes my heart,
of my shame, of all my meager bliss—
only letters sealed in a book.

Once the wave vanishes, who will believe
in its mighty force which does not return—
even if on the sand's pale surface one can still see
a sign of its touch, feeble and feathery?

My love cast ashore its corals,
and fishermen who happened along
collected them and carried them far away—

a bored stranger now touches them,
and in a hurried and fleeting world
Time will toy with them like a small boy.

You Are Wondrous

I
You are wondrous, wholly wondrous
joy of my heart. Of all my sins
perhaps God will punish me for this one
on Judgment Day. And I have no excuse.

It was given to me for free, not as payment
for my agonies, not reward for the bitterness.
Light of a sudden dawn opened my eyes
and I understood my dream, clear as day.

In an angry and unbending world,
under cold skies
I stand and in my heart, joy.

Foolish bird, how have you built a nest
in a dead rock! To whom will your voice carry
psalms of your beloved, song of your bliss?

2

By law I am not entitled
to this joy. I know, by law
I do not deserve the splendor of bridal clothes
but the sackcloth of the penitent.

But I am guilty that at my journey's end,
my eyes toward the wasteland,
happiness caught me like a downpour
and I had no time to cover my head.

Ever since I have been like a tree in the heart of the desert
on which a thousand birds have descended,
its dry branches filling with song.

Ever since I have been a pool in the heart of night—
in their randomness, generous skies
have scattered in it all the stars.

A Night Psalm

The crescent moon is draped in black,
all the stars are hidden from sight,
from the North to far Yemen
there is not a single ray of light.

And morning, faithful widower,
clutches a grey sack tight,
from the North to far Yemen
not a single ray of light.

O please, light a white candle
in the black tent of my heart,
from the North to far Yemen
let there be light.

From the Songs of My Beloved Land

I

My motherland, beautiful and poor—
the Queen has no home, the King no crown.
Seven days of spring a year
rain and chill all the rest.

But for seven days the roses bloom,
for seven days the dewdrops shine,
for seven days the windows are open,
and all your beggars stand in the street
turning their pale faces to the good light,
and all your beggars are content.

My motherland, beautiful and poor—
the Queen has no home, the King no crown,
only seven holidays a year
work and hunger all the rest.

But for seven days the candles are blessed,
for seven days the tables are set,
for seven days the hearts are open,
and all your beggars stand at prayer,
and your daughters and sons are bride and groom,
and all your beggars are brothers.

My wretched one, bitter and poor,
the King has no home, the Queen no crown—
only one in the world speaks your praise
shame and disgrace all the rest.

And so I'll walk to every street and corner,
every market and yard, alley and park,
and from the ruins of your walls I'll gather
every small stone as keepsake.

And from town to town, country to country
I'll wander with music and song
to tell of your radiant poverty.

2
In the land of my love the almond tree blossoms,
in the land of my love they await a visitor,
seven maidens,
seven mothers,
seven brides at the gate.

In my beloved land there's a flag on the tower,
to my beloved land the pilgrim will wander
in a goodly time,
in a blessed hour,
in a moment that erases all sorrow.

But who has eagle eyes and will see them,
who a wise heart and will know them,
who will not err
who not mistake,
who, but who, will open the gate?

I sleep and my heart is awake,
the visitor passes by my house.
Morning dawns

and in the yard
one lonely stone is overturned.

3
In the poor land that I love
even the moon in the sky
stands at the doorway like a pauper
hesitant, pale and bent.

And the clouds, torn and tattered,
come from the corner of the sky,
graceful and modest and hurrying
to cover its impoverished shame.

In the morning the sun rises
yellow as autumn's eye
and at the alley's entrance lies
the golden rooster, slain.

from
Last Words (1959)

From the Songs of Zion

1. Night
Did a golden bell chime in the high heavens?
Did a dew-drop touch the top of the cypress?
Sing for us from the songs of Zion!
How shall we sing a song of Zion in the land of Zion
when we have not even begun to listen?

2. The Quarry
Stubborn, deaf, mute
this stone in its refusal.
Still, still, still,
the secrets of its heart.

Until your quarrying hand touched it
and, wounded and broken,
it abandons its secret and speaks
happiness and pain,
and its voice—
love.

3. Olive Trees
They withstood the heat wave
and were confidants of the storm—
as though they had stationed themselves for eternity
on the slope across from the ruined village,
where they silvered in the cool light of the crescent moon.

Stand still, how abundant in this peace.
Here is ripe old age!
Listen, listen to the gusts
of wind through the landscape of olives.
What modest trees!
Can you hear? They are speaking now
wise and simple things.

4. Migrating Birds

That same spring morning
the sky sprouted wings.
And in its wandering westward
the breathing sky spoke
the Traveler's Prayer:
"O God,
bring us safely
across the ocean
across the deep waters,
and in autumn return us
to this little country
which has heard all our songs."

On Nightmares' Trail

I

And if I forget the prayer?
And if strangled weeping from behind
a locked door breaches the first gate?
No, no, better I should stay awake.
I cannot sleep, I cannot—

And if the windows are open
and the gloom from within darkened
rooms breaks into day?
And if I forget the prayer?

The path always, always, leads
to this place. Always, always.
But there was witchcraft, there was a word—
my lips cannot remember the prayer.

2

You tell me that this fire
does not burn, that you walk
through my night's flames unharmed.

"I cannot hear," you say,
"this voice of weeping. Your dream is mute.
You are the dreamer and I the one awake."

Tall and whole, you walk
among my thorns unharmed.
All is sealed and my dream is mute.
I want to cry out, cry out, cry out—

Last Words

1

I am cold to my bones. The landscape before me
is like a torn cloak. With a weary hand
I write down
the last line of a poem.
Already in the eighth century
on the banks of the yellow river
there sat a poet who knew
the last word.

2

What will our end be? The skies
stand still.
Were it not for the clock's ticking
we wouldn't know
how far we already are
from morning.
What seed will the winds carry in spring?
What flower
will grow on our graves?
I pray
it is a yellow buttercup.
In days gone by
I picked one on the hills.
What will our end be?

3
What will our end be?
Two boys in the street
sing a song.
In two windows above the street
lights are already lit.
Two boats in the port
set sail tonight.
My two hands in your hands
are cold.
What will our end be?

4
What will our end be? Night's omens
are beautiful, but obscure. The wind
rolls the silver hoop through the skies.
Ancient moon! How they all mistook you—
the innocent lovers and the sages of Egypt.
Now silence has passed its sentence.
And we
what will our end be?

5
The pain
is as clear as the light of day.
Above any doubt,
as perfect as faith.

Three Days

1

I stand in the heart of the desert
without even a single star above me
and the wind does not speak to me
and the sands will not preserve my footsteps.

2

I cried out: "Answer me!"
No one answered.
I knocked: "Open!"
No one opened.
Outside the evening was scorching and pale.
I went to knock on another gate.

I cried out: "Answer me!"
No one answered.
I knocked: "Open!"
No one opened.
Outside night was blind and breathless.
I went to knock on another gate.

I whispered: "Answer me!"
No one answered.
I pleaded: "Open!"
No one opened.
In a dewless morning the sun rose
and there the city watchmen found me.

3
For three days his memory would not leave me
and on the fourth day I sliced the bread
and on the fourth day I opened my window
and on the fourth day I saw the sea.

And on the fourth day I knew
the sea is very beautiful, its expanse blue
and in the salty gust of wind—
the scent of the sea, not the taste of my tears.

The Lovers on the Beach

He:
Your nearness and the sea's
have stolen my sleep.
Your breath drawn salty from the sea
has invaded my house.
And the waves wild
weeping all the while
surge to the heights of my love.
Come to me, my bride—

In a red moon above the sea
your blood flows.
In a red moon above the sea
my blood and yours.
And the waves wild
weeping all the while
cry out your name, your name, your name.
Come to me, my bride.

How can I close my window
and the storm is near?
How can I close my window
and your feet are bare?
How can I close my window
and the sea calls out?
How can I close my window
and you are awake?
And the owl of night's heart
has torn my sleep in two?
Come to me, my bride.

She:
You sent the owl
to rouse me from sleep.
You taught me to scream
words of love and beseeching—
but I'll not come, not come, not come!

You set loose in me the scent
of seaweed and full moons,
you commanded the sea to moan
in the voice of love and beseeching—
but I'll not come, not come, not come!

The waves kissed my legs,
the hem of my white dress.
In your voice of love and beseeching
they said: "Come to me."
And I returned home,
I shut my door,
my window is sealed—
my heart sleeps and I sleep.

From My Mother's House

I
My mother's mother died
in the spring of her days. And her daughter
did not remember her face. Her image
engraved on my grandfather's heart
was erased from the world of images
after his death.

Only her mirror remained in the house,
grown deeper with age in its silver frame.
And I, her pale granddaughter, who look nothing like her,
peer into it today as though into
a lake hiding its treasures
deep under the water.

Deep down, behind my eyes,
I see a young woman
pink-cheeked and smiling.
A wig on her head.
She is hanging
a long earring on her ear-lobe. Threading it through
the slender crevice in the tender flesh
of her ear.

Deep down, behind my eyes, the light
golden flecks of her eyes shine.
And the mirror testifies to the family
tradition:
that she was very beautiful.

2

Apples like these, my mother says,
your grandfather picked in his garden in the fall.
Apples like these, my mother says,
didn't grow even in the mayor's yard.

Eighty-two years old, my mother says,
he pruned the apple-branches by himself.
On the top of a ladder, my mother says,
erect and strong among the tree-tops.

Apples like these, my mother says...
and I close my eyes slowly
and I see the garden his hands planted,
and a wide white beard, all grandeur,
peeking out and glowing from the green of the leaves.

Apples like these—

Splinters of a Storm

1. If Not for the Wind

If not for the wind we could hear
our voices. Then we would know
what fear night planted in our hearts
and what longing alarmed us with morning.
But the wind comes and the wind goes
and the wind carries away all voices.
If our faces had not turned so white
we could see the wind's pale path.

2. Uprooted Tree

It was wrenched from its roots, its core.
Now it will lie here until evening—
until porters come to carry it away
to someplace-no-one-wants-it greenleaf-branch.

How lucky no bird built a nest in it.
How lucky that this storm
has destroyed no other innocent dreams.
Blessed are the solitary in their deaths!

Now all its springs and all its autumns
will travel with it to an unknown land.
And on another treetop a foolish bird
will sing hymns to its eternal joy.

3. The Wise Men Will Testify

The wise men will testify that the sun
still shines somewhere in the heavens,
for somewhere behind the black clouds
light's eternity will not lie.
The wise men know this.
But in the children's eyes today—
only lightning's afterimage
and the echo of thunder.

4. Today the Gardeners are Sad

Today the gardeners are sad,
but the farmers
bless the rain.
And we two
at a loss
hide from each other
our eyes.
Let's be wise: don't ask
what grew, what withered,
what was uprooted from the heart.

This storm
will soon pass,
this question
will soon be forgotten.
See, there's a rainbow already
above the tower.

Today the gardeners are sad,
but the farmers
bless the rain.

5. Next Day

The green today is very green.
And the grey today is very grey.
A bit of black, and no white in the city.
The unquiet today are very unquiet.
And the past today—very past.
A bit of future. And no present in the air.

And it's still not easy to breathe, and it's still not easy
to think facing this entangled wind.
And it's not at all simple to wait.
The storm touches eyelashes,
and shatters every moment to pieces.
But the green today is very green.

Illuminations

I

And so you go out into the streets
of the city which is always your city,
to see things in which there is not
a trace of anything new.

And so you walk in the street,
passing by houses and stores,
passing faces and smiles
and old beggars.

And every face reminds you:
You've already seen it!
And all the voices tell you:
You heard them yesterday too.

But suddenly at the end of the street
there stands a single blue lamp
which stood there yesterday too
and all of a sudden there it stands.

And there is no knowing what happened,
no explanation for the blue light
no explanation for the windows
in the house nearby.

But evening has the wing of a dove
and it spreads over the city, sheltering
windows and smiles
and old beggars.

2
Over one of the hills
flies an orange bird
whose name I do not know.
But the olive trees know her
and the wind, chasing her, sings:
Here is your home.

In the eyes of a small Arab girl
at the edge of the ruined village
hovers an orange bird
whose name I do not know.

3
Have you seen the rain? We are quiet.
Three angels from an ancient tale
are walking slowly among the houses and trees.

Nothing has changed. Only the rain
taps cautiously on the stone. The street glows.
We see how they cross the road
three angels from an ancient tale.

The door is open. The flour sifted.
The rain is quiet, for the miracle
has already happened.

from
With this Night (1964)

With this Night

With this night and all its silences
With this night—
with three stars
lost between the trees
with this wind.

With this wind
that has stopped to listen
to this night—
with this night
and three stars
and this wind.

The Shortest Journey

1. Tel Aviv 1935

Then the aerials on the city's roofs were
like the masts of Columbus' ships
and every raven that perched on their tips
announced a new continent.

And the kit-bags of travelers walked the streets
and the language of a foreign land
cut through the heat of the day
like the blade of a cold knife.

How could the air of the small city
bear so many
childhood memories, wilted loves,
rooms which were emptied somewhere?

Like pictures blackening in a camera
the clear cold nights reversed,
rainy summer nights across the sea
and shadowy mornings of great cities.

And the sound of footsteps behind your back
drum the marching songs of foreign troops,
and it seems—if you but turn your head
there is your hometown church floating on the sea.

2. Evening in the Café

The city in a many-colored robe
of the balconies' awnings
and clear wine in lanterns
and cloudy light in the glasses.

Splinters of argument and spilling
voices, dishes. Nearby lights
erase an ancient reckoning of stars
on the black slate of night.

The sea behind our backs
with impatient diligence
counts and counts our heart beats
in an autumnal pact with my clock.

Only the very young know
the value of time and its meaning
with its lost nights
with all we lose
in moments that pass by wasted.

And on the pavement across the way
like a not-to-be-believed nightmare
an old man slowly, quietly, walks by—
he has no reason to hurry.

3. A Rainy Autumn Night and a Clear Morning

Into a dark and sealed night
where only the jackals
know its alleyways
a city was tossed.

Dressed in white
undefended
before the rain's lash
the thunder's rebuke
the caress of an old sea's lust.

Our little city
we and our lives
are hers—

But the clear morning has opened her prison gates
and behold—

More dark circles under her damp lashes—
she is white and uncomely
without a past, without pride—
how beautiful was her youth!

4. Then She Had

Then she still had the scent of sea,
of shells, orange peelings and pre-summer sirocco,
and the magic of an uncertain
familiarity, like a dream twice dreamt.

Light and sea surrounded her. A hundred hoops
held in her the taste of salty longings—

My thirsty sands, my yearning youth,
all my crowned sorrows contemptible of the kingdom—
and the city a white island on green waves.

5. I Walked Then

I walked then
as though someone loves me very much.
On earth's surface the debris of ruins laughed
and a wind in the mighty heavens.

I walked then
as though someone dreamed me beautiful.
On night's surface deep waters blossomed
and the sea's mirror sketched for me my face
as though someone wrote poems about me.

I walked and reached silence.
And then it seems something began.

6. The Shortest Journey

The shortest journey is the one across years.
The light is not yet spent. The house has fallen. The wall
has moved.
And here they stand side by side like neighbors
my night of now, my day of then.
What words do they exchange: we change, we age?

The shortest journey is the one into the past.
Remember? Cool sea-waters, two boats embracing,
children on the hilltop raising torches—
We age? We change? Believe me, I still have
very long hours until tomorrow.

Songs of a Foreign Woman

I

I am green and replete like a song that has passed through the grass
I am soft and deep like a bird's nest.
I am from long ago,
from a forest that taught me to breathe
from the languor of lovers asleep in the grass
locked in each other's arms.

I am from there—
from the village of small winds.
On the last hilltop there stood a windmill
and the sky hung on its wings clouds mixed with smoke.
And the wind came and the wind went.
I am from a village beating a rhythm on wooden spoons
I am from there.

2

Windmill, windmill,
on what shore did the seagulls
call out the name of my dead country?
Windmill, windmill.

On what road did the travelers walk
feeling the sunset kingdom on their backs
and not turning around?
Wings fluttered in the wind.

Where
is the garden red with autumn

that covered its shadows
and hid twilight in its leaves
and let the wind pass through?

And the wind called out with the seagull
the name of my dead country—
and here I am, free and silent.
Windmill, windmill!

3
Land of low winds, I was yours,
my heart holding every drop of your rain.
I walk with uncertain legs—no angel will hold me up—
to bring your forests' wild mushrooms to the Kingdom of Heaven.

In my Kingdom of Heaven they still remember your feast days.
A joyous harmonica plays the songs of the dead.
One star entangled in the wings of the windmill
turns round and round—
and I have grown old and grey and no one will dance with me.

Still, I will come to the feast, for the gate is open.
I'll slip off my shoes and sit in the shade.
My face will flow gently in the waters of the lazy stream,

my face from the shores of your rivers,
illuminated with the memory of you—
Windmill, windmill.

A Nameless Journey

1

Where am I? How can I explain where I am?
My eyes are not visible in any window.
My face is not reflected in any mirror.
All the city's streetcars ride on without me.

And the rain falls and does not wet my hands.
And I am here, wholly here—
in a foreign city
in the heart of a great foreign homeland.

2

My room is so small
that the days in it are wary and grow shorter,
and I too live in it cautiously
in the smell of smoke and apples.

At night the neighbors light a lamp:
across a great courtyard, through the high birch leaves,
a window facing me glows quietly.
Sometimes at night it's hard to remember
that once
somewhere—
there was a window which was mine.

3

It's been weeks since anyone has addressed me
by name, and it's so simple:

the parrots in my kitchen
haven't yet learned it,
people in all corners of the city
don't know it.
It exists only on paper, in writing,
it has no sound, no note or voice.

For days I walk nameless
in the street whose name I know.
For hours I sit nameless
facing a tree whose name I know.
Sometimes, nameless, I think
of he whose name I do not know.

4
I walked with the boats and I stood with the bridges
and I was cast on the street
with the falling elm leaves,
I had an autumn
and I had a cloud of light beside a black chimney.
And I had a strange name
which no one can guess.

Aug.–Sept. 1960, Copenhagen

A Look at a Bee

1

In the lit-up window square—
on the pane, from outside,
the silhouette of a bee—
you can hardly see her wings.

Upside down.
Narrow body.
Six thin legs—
with nakedness exposed,
with ugly menace,
a bee crawls.

How can we crown her with songs of praise?
How can we sing and what?
A small child will come and say:
The Queen has no clothes.

2

She was a golden leaf falling in the sunlight,
she was a drop of dark honey on the flower,
and a drop of dew in the swarm of stars—
and here she is a shadow.

A solitary word of song in the buzzing swarm,
a declaration of diligence in the lazy heat,
a flash of light in the ashes of dusk—
and here she is a shadow.

from With this Night (1964)

3
Your honey? Who will remember your honey?
It's there, far off, in the hive.
Here, on the lit-up window pane, your body, your head—
all of you stinger, hatred that is impotent, miserable and blind.
Fear kills.
        Protect yourself.

From the Songs of Two Autumns

1

Somewhere something somebody there—
black dawn and dark granite sails.
The river, the leaves in their rustling fall,
song of the forest.
I pass by—

I pass by like this autumn
setting its foot on first fragile ice
thin and dark and falling
to be buried in the cold rain of a black dawn.

I pass by like this star
falling slowly into light-no-light
behind the erased horizon,
there to meet a different night.

2

I pass by like this pain
leaving my body,
the joy of departure
as from this pain
leaving my body.

I part from myself
as does this autumn—
from the swans of its black dawn
and from its winged clouds.

I pass without sorrow the borders of change.
Tomorrow
the snow on the lovely footpath will wrap in silence
my life,
my body that ached,
the autumn,
the flight of my black swans.

3
Here autumn is the border of spring
and the cypress is an eternal flame.
Do not see me as fleeting
for the cypress is an eternal flame.

In the vineyard the leaves have fallen,
in the hills the wild onion flowers have bloomed.
Do not see me as fleeting
a black candle burns in the hills.

The grave is hewn in the hills.
The grass is soft like a flock of sheep.
Do not see me as fleeting
for the cypress is an eternal flame.

And a Third Autumn

1
Thorns. Rocks. Thistles. I walked
over the stones. A horizon of thorns,
endless thorns—earth of bramble and dry-bush
and foreign birds alighting.

And foreign birds—their sharp voice
and the sting of summer. An autumn of stones,
edges of the sky so bright.
An autumn of heat waves. The rain still far off.

Among the thorns dark gold lies hidden.
Among the thorns the voice of foreign birds.
Among the thorns toward a thorny horizon
the days walk weary as beggars.

2
Dead earth and a living sky
a breathing stone and a still wind
open space and ruins—

My thirsty youth—
what a trampled and desolate road!
What chill is plotting our death
in the hiding places of the days to come.

For One Who Does Not Believe

I

For one who does not believe
it's hard to live this year—
the fields ask for a blessing
the sea asks for faith
and you—you ask for nothing.

My heart sleeps its sleep
and I sleep.
My dream is heavy with silence
and my dead walk in my sleep
as in an ancient fortress.
How will I wake from my sleep
when my heart has no faith
and you ask for nothing?

2

You ask for nothing—
not for this tree
that has stood these ten years
like a sentry at his post,

not for this path
that at the end of ten years
has reached my doorstep,
not for the clear image
in the lake of my sleep.

You ask for nothing—

with the open eyes of a blind man
boats pass by
and the sea keeps a vow of silence.
And one bird
longs to rend the desert's
slumber.
And you long for nothing.

3
Only the hills are already awake
and the walls and their mosses.
Tear my sleep from me.
Try to wake me.

A lonely dawn stands over me
an echo-less dawn.
Let it lean over me
let it weep over me
for the dawn has returned to me,
prodigal son!

Only the hills are already awake
and I sleep.
Dawn presses up to my window-pane
and calls out my name
and I do not answer.

Passed to Another World

I

They've passed to another world
and that now is their world
but my heart is starving
in this world:

to hunger in his hunger
to be quenched in his thirst
to blossom in the blossoming
of his seed and root

and to love him
and to despise him
but to be always within
his envy and his fears.

2

And you walked among the dead
and there were many dead there
and you searched for a living soul—
there was not a living soul there.

And the faces of the dead were
free of pain and free of worry—
and you asked for one grace only:
the grace of suffering.

Remember me fondly
for I was your sorrow,

for I was always
your living well-of-suffering.

But I am already with the dead
and my face is like the faces of the dead,
and my face, like theirs, is quiet
free of pain and free of worry.

3
At the Holy Gate
stands the Watchman
and no one from within the Temple
comes out to meet me.

For in the Temple sit
all your dear friends
and there is no room left
for the others who love you.

For even on the day you died
another was with you
and my name is not inscribed
in the Book of your Kingdom.

4
Ten years after your death
I'll know without doubt that I loved you,
or ten years after my death
you'll know without doubt that you've forgotten me.
And these are small and simple things
inscribed in the Book of the Dead.

God Once Commanded Us

God once commanded us to stand strong and steadfast
under the terrible Tree of Life.
And we stood, stricken with expectations, in a black wind of
                                                        years—
perhaps the fruit would drop at our feet?
And nothing happened.

And on the day of secret reckoning
between Him and us
we saw a bent landscape and brown leaves falling
and the wind still blowing in our faces.

Then, a small voice said: this is your Day of Liberation.
That's all. And it is good.

Now I walk alone toward the blade of cutting cold
just a few paces
to that fading light
in the dark angle of the street.

Portrait of the Poet as an Old Man

I

I sit at my desk
and boys play on my grave.
I sign my last poem
and they erase my name and my memory,
and no one will know anymore that I
am a morning-bird—the lark:
they say I was always a cricket
singing in the dark corners.

2

Why don't you stop, fool,
combining cursed words?
Why don't you stop, fool,
polishing short lines?

You're alone and the city sleeps
and around you silence,
and your poems come like an old lady
with a tale of her beauty
and a dress that is long out-of-style…
—but I still love her.

3

Don't try to follow the new generation,
the new generation doesn't want you,
the new generation is going somewhere else
and you don't have an invitation.

from With this Night (1964)

Don't try to follow the new generation,
the new generation doesn't want you.
The new generation wants only to bury you
and to bequeath you to other generations.

Far Away

1. Even this Landscape

Even this landscape
does not want to hear
the beautiful words
with which I've adorned it;
even this handsome tree
commands me to be silent and is fearful
lest I transgress with my tongue.

I had similar names
and your name leaning into the rock,
I had names that echoed
and your name rustling in the trees.
I had many names
but I never spoke the one Name
and now
I'll not transgress with my tongue
lest the echo reply.

2. And Of All the Dead

Far away—
and no one asks anything of me.
He who took an oath
is broken
and he who was taken prisoner
never returned.

And of all the dead
who lifted their faces toward me

there was not even one
who wanted me to weep over him.

3. It is Not the Sea

It is not the sea that stands between us,
it is not the abyss that stands between us,
it is not time that stands between us
it is—we, the two of us, who stand between us.

4. Far Away

Far away
from everything—
from the lovely houses
on the city streets
from the floating leaf
from the key word
wise men inscribed on parchment.

Far away—
I walked with the boats
and I stood with the bridges
I cross the borders of change without sorrow.
My love—
far now
from that one
perfect day
I've always remembered.
Far from my eyes
that saw clouds and a world.

Within my body that knows no answer.

Within this light
that kills the other light
not yet extinguished.

5. Answer

Desire nothing
and mourn nothing
and what you have cried over
is already gone.

Toward Myself

The years have made up my face
with memories of love
and have adorned my hair with light silver threads
making me most beautiful.

In my eyes
landscapes are reflected.
And the paths I have trod
have straightened my stride—
tired and lovely steps.

If you should see me now
you would not recognize your yesterdays—
I am walking toward myself
bearing the face you searched for in vain
when I was walking toward you.

from
The Remains of Life (1978)

*

A young poet suddenly falls silent
for fear of telling the truth.
An old poet falls silent for fear
the best in a poem
is its lie.

＊

And the poem I did not write
when I was writing poems
I still remember it all
every word, every sound.
And it will remain unwritten even now.

If I had written it then,
it would have been too naked a truth.
And if I were to write it now
it would be a total lie.

Come, descend upon me, O Muse,
rest your whitening head
upon my shoulder.

We'll play with words—

How lucid the world is in this new game—

not then, not now
not truth, not lies

the two sides of the scale rise and fall
to a steady beat.

*

In everything there is at least an eighth part
that is death. Its weight is not great.
With what secret and carefree grace
we carry it everywhere we go.
On lovely awakenings, on journeys,
in lovers' words, in our distraction
forgotten at the edges of our affairs
it is always with us. Weighing
hardly anything at all.

from Fragments

*

Only one step.
You will not fall into the depths.
Hard earth
without the mercy of the abyss
...

*

Already the silences are easy.
The light is bright.
When there are no roads
there is no fear of borders.
And there is nothing to reveal
when there is nothing to hide.
...

On the Mount of Olives

A landscape like this has no answers
when aging people
stand on the road
and a summer day passes them by
as by the broken stones
in this place.

Jerusalem, Earthly and Heavenly

1
Break your bread in two,
Jerusalem, earthly and heavenly,
thorn jewels on your slopes
and your sun among the thistles.
A hundred deaths but not your mercy!
Break your bread in two:
one part for the birds of the sky
the other
for heavy feet to trample
at the crossroads.

2
People are walking in the pretend city.
Its sky passed over like a shadow
and no one trembled.
In the alley's descent
its lofty past conceals itself.

Poor children sing
in indifferent voices:
"David King of Israel
lives on forever."

3
Above my house
one late swallow
all the migrating birds
have already returned north.

Above my eyes
toward evening
in a city weary of wanderings
in the wayfarers' quarter
small and trembling
wings
trace circles of despair.

A Hebron-glass-sky.
First lamp that is lit.
A swallow with no nest.
Flight that has stopped.

What now?

*

The clasp of sand and stone
Hagar's,
Antigone's,
mine.

The clasp of sand and stone.
The tight-lipped love,
the downcast pride,
the proud insult.

On the exiles' path
the clasp of sand and stone—
the sky near by—
and in the sky
star cacti.

*

The day turned.
It was not always so.
The day turned its back on me—
my night is an eternal flame.
Now the poems will come
mercilessly.
And I won't know what to say.
My last love.
Where am I?
So it will be
so it will always be.

*

My entire life summed up in that one moment—
a light-ray on a deer's antler.
The branches broken. In the forest's darkness
the light-ray trampled under my foot.

*

There were questions
and answers called into question.
There were duplicate stones
for every desire.
A land of lamentations
and a vast sun
and rejoicing at its sorrows on the nights
a flawed moon rose.

A Hike in the Hills

for Tuvia Ruebner

1

Last climb in the bronze hills.
I remembered nothing
        only that my eyes were filled with autumn.
And my lips
blackened by the forest's berries
were left wordless.
But the hills
from the coolness of the sky
and from the heart of the lake
spoke silence to me
beautifully.

2

Our loves are not many.
Passing by we tried
to smile at the pine trunks
and at the hills' green stone.
And waiting for no reply we walked on
so happy
with all that is not ours,
and is not with us
and does not forget
for it does not remember.

3
My snow was light-blue
and yours
pale green.
My part of the sky—
yellowish bottle-glass,
and yours—
faded parchment of an ancient prayer.
In your lake—peaks.
In mine—geese.
I will write one poem
and you another.
But we will be silent together
on the same path.

Small Poems

1. Somewhere in Samaria

(Somewhere in Samaria I picked wildflowers
—Gogol)

I picked a wildflower and tossed it away. I waited
two days in the rain at a forgotten station.
My God, you'll never believe in me again! I passed by
so close and didn't recognize you.

2. At the Small Station

At night the boxcars passed by. I didn't raise my eyes.
What could I possibly see in the glow of their fleeting light?
I should have known: this train
doesn't stop at the small station.

3. All of Night's Stars

All of night's large stars remain there.
The heavens belong to God.
My regrets are not lovely.
My clouds are low.

4. A Yellow Leaf

I am not in the desert. There is a clock here
and I'm afraid of arriving late.
Here the wind carries a yellow leaf
and brings it to my doorway.
I am not in the desert.

5. Another Measure of Distance

Another measure of distance. Another tomorrow and another.
And what will I say then? And to whom?
And how will I render judgment when no witnesses remain?
I was a gate on the border
where the leave-takers stood.

*

The hills today are shadows of hills
the silence an echo of silence.
Today I set out on my way
and the sound of my steps is not heard.

Today I set out on my way
and the sound of my steps is not heard.

*

But it was a wondrous spring
tiny silver fish swam in your eyes
and the image of your eyes swam in my eyes
and we could sink: fathom after fathom—
tiny silver fish have disappeared from your eyes.

Nightmare

At the moment it was decreed I shouldn't wait
I had almost managed also to forget.
To count empty hours, endless
without hope of rest—
and how will I know if this is the moon?
Wake me, I'm not asleep.

Tomorrow? But yesterday was a tomorrow too.
No one appealed, and thus silence was set.
Only from a distance I heard a parched voice—
and so it is today. Suddenly a year has passed by.
Wake me, I'm not asleep.

Almost to forget. Only one hour
from the day's hours always chokes me.
Slit throat, like a slaughtered chicken.
Here it fell. And again silence is set.
Everything foretold. Truth and faith.
Wake me. I'm not asleep.

*

Yes, I have more
more beautiful still,
more precious still,
I have more:
words of adornment
and wisdom
and extravagance
and words of truth.

Were it not for the surrender
and the perfect
knowledge
I would set them before you
like an enchanted necklace of islands.

*

Of all your forgotten ones I
am the most forgotten.
Of all the faces
you have seen in the mirror
my face
is the most transparent.
And my voice
is lower than a cut field. And my name
is engraved on a heavy stone
at the bottom of the well.

*

I'll rise, I will rise
from my sleep
in a different spirit,
in a different land
where there is no love.

The shining morning birds
on barbed fences

I knew, I've forgotten.
I have forgotten.
I am other.
I am other.
I am free.

I am as free as the water torrent,
fresh and never aging,
never aging, I live on

a hundred years and one night.

On the Dangers of Smoking

A rainy morning. Don't get up. Don't smoke, don't
even read too much. What a strange spring!
What a strange spring. A type of morning darkness...
Don't read too much. What a cloudy spring!

You used to complain. Did it help? Did you bring back your dead?
The pain of the body, of the newspaper, of the song. Of the Song-
of-Songs.
Silence the better part of wisdom? Perhaps. Lucky we've since
learned
not to wake neighbors, not bother friends.

A rainy morning. Don't get up. Night passed quietly.
Night passed. And now—what a cloudy spring!
A morning like night. That's good. Only the silence stifles.
What a heavy spring! I told you: don't smoke.

The Remains of Life

1

I strode into this night
which is endless
and suddenly it was morning
and the sun lit up
the faces of the living
who envied the dead.

2

"The remains of life," he said,
"the remains of life are wisdom or folly—
and the choice is yours."

3

Ten times
maybe twenty
I passed this place
in peace.
But who's to say
that today
I'll pass this place
in peace.

4
Snow fell
and in a foreign land
there was a war
and they died in the snow
(as they do here in the spring)
in a foreign land.

5
We were very young
and very poor
our lives a patchwork.
We read books
and in the evening we went dancing—
and sometimes we were even
happy.

6
We were young without hope
we grew up without faith
we grow old without complaint.

Sickness

The world still stands its ground
and stands my ground.
Someone
has pasted on my window pane
a piece of the sky
and my neighbor's Venetian blind.

But at night
the world stands its ground
alone.
And I
walk away from it
over the depths of my memory.

White Poplar Leaves

1

White poplar leaves
illuminated in the dark hush
and all the birds keeping quiet
the evening hours.
How did you manage
to find yourself shelter
on an island without
even a single dream?

2

In the purified silence
empty
is the name that echoed in vain.
In the isolated silence
holding fast
to the one name.
In the silence of glass
thin to near breaking
the one name in silence
grows and grows stronger.

3
Farewell to me, farewell
and do not pray for my well-being—
farewell to me, farewell,
and do not ask for whom—
I am lost in a deep peace
my ears are sealed
and my face
floats on the surface of silence.

*

Tomorrow I will die.
Tomorrow you will see
what was my face
what were my eyes.

When tomorrow arrives you
will come to my house's edge
to pay last respects
and divide up the spoils.

Tomorrow all will be
yours and for you.
Tomorrow you are right
in everything you say.

But today I
stand at the threshold
and I'll cross over my border
and no one may trespass.

*

And this will be the judgment.
And thus will be the judgment
and on the day of judgment
there will be justice in the judgment

And we will not know
and we will not understand.
And we will stand mute
before the justice of the judgment.
And this will be the judgment.

And those who die by judgment,
they will be witnesses of the judgment,
all who have died since then
and those who die now.

They will attest to the judgment,
and their testimony will be true.
For they and the living
for they are justification of the judgment.
And this will be the judgment.

Uncollected Poems

Those Who Knew Me Will Remember

Those who knew me will remember:
"She desired the earthly life
an abundance of darkness, a bit of light.
She loved the moon-ray shattering against the window's glass
and the pre-spring fragrance of linden buds,
and neighborly talk in the coffee-house dust,
where in a dream of friendship phrase nestles phrase.
And the great loneliness of foreign and despised cities
and the many people who loved her just a little,
some who walked away alone and forgot her name,
some who longed to love her and didn't know how...
She was sad and all her days lived the pain
of life's great joy…"

Those who remember me will know:
"She was lonely
and like every person she was woven from darkness and light
and there is almost nothing to remember—"

*

My hands are pale
like pre-dawn stars—
so foreign
are my fingers to the hand
like day which has become
already evening—
after the singing of joyous words
a drawn-out silence
and wine goblets
falling still
like a pause
in the flow of a tune close by
and so different.

And on the hand
a ring
like a Sabbath window
where candles mother failed to light look out.
Perhaps tonight
I—quite simply—
will cry in the streets
into the soul
inward…

Khamsin

I
All the shutters in my room are closed
heat and darkness have sealed here a pact.
Like a Passover *seder* in the house of Marranos
the breakfast meal is set.

You slice bread for me: "Eat, eat!"
Your beautiful hand is shriveled.
From morning till night you toil for me
all to forget your own fatigue.

Mother, forgive me, you couldn't solve, couldn't know,
that my country—land of heat-waves—is barren and hard,
that the day here is cruel like the silence of the daughter
who matured and became a woman.

2
And tomorrow again the throat's suffocation.
Night and heat. You and she.
Tomorrow every moment will be the last
in time—the divine suicide.

A heavy laughter will hurt, will hurt—
heat. You and she. And there is no escape.
A cold shudder carves through the dry winds:
a hundred deaths and not this one envy!

Ne'ilah / Closing

1. The Sun Will Turn

This naked sun knows
my shame less than the darkness
of nights which bathed in my dreams.

We watch each other
shamelessly
accustomed to the painted smile
and to the yielding
that masquerades
as courage.

Only in the August afternoon, its light
tells me the truth
and I cast down my eyes.

No matter—
soon,
the sun will turn.
And night
will work wonders
caressing
the scars of my shame.

2. Because the Day Fades

During the day I never cried. And
at night
in the cage of my lonely shame
I was never granted
the grace of tears.
Only at the passing of the eighth day
when the last dove
deserted the square,
and the voices of boys shrank
before the signposts of dusk,
I returned home, unclear
of my footsteps' path.
And when I asked a stranger
directions and I saw
in his eyes the surprise of embarrassed
pity, I understood
I was walking in the street
and crying.

And my pain was not eased.

3. Open for Us a Gate

One after another things
are happening to me which
at another time would light up in me
all the lamplights of joy.
And I would walk then lovely,
careful, lest they be extinguished,
carrying back and forth
humble thanksgiving.

But in this setting
they are summer's flashes,
sparks—
and when they vanish
the clouds are even darker
and in the stifling air
there is no expectation of rain.

Heaven stands sealed.
Open for us a gate.

4. *Ne'ilah*

I was never taught how to stand in prayer.
Up in the women's section
there was one woman who lifted her voice
above words and meanings
sealed before her
and her God.

With all the many killed, she has long since been forgotten.
And I, in another land,
want to shout out like her
but cannot:
I do not remember
how to speak to dead angels
at the hour the gates are closing.

Notes on the Poems

The poem *About Myself*, placed here as an epigraph to the entire collection, is from Goldberg's 1964 collection *With this Night*.

> ❧

Early Poems (1935–1942)

The poems in this section are taken from *Smoke Rings* (1935), *The Green-Eyed Stalk* (1940) and *From My Old Home* (1942).

Pietà

Stanza 3: In the original, the twice repeated "Pietà" is written in English. I have written the words in italics to signal this shift in voice.

Childhood

1. Opening

Line 6—Literally, "and there was song" (*va'yehee mizmor*). Cf. Genesis 1:3—"and there was light" (*va'yehee or*) and Genesis 1: 5—"and there was evening and there was morning, the first day" (*va'yehee erev va'yehee boker yom rishon*). This formulaic proclamation of existence is repeated at the end of each day in the creation week, as described in Genesis.

Citations from the Bible are taken from both the Jewish Publication Society translation and the King James Version.

Lines 10–12—Literally, "and dew / and clover / and lamb." The forceful alliterative link between the three words in the Hebrew original (*tal, tiltan, taleh*) is recreated in the dew/daisy/dove link of the translation. I have allowed myself this liberty, in part, because the lamb and the dove traditionally share the attributes of innocence, purity and peacefulness.

2. The Beach

In Goldberg's three-volume *The Collected Poems* (Sifriat Poalim 1973/1986) published posthumously, this section comes third in the series and there is a second section entitled "Night." However, in the selected poems of *Early and Late* (1959/2003) which Goldberg herself edited, Goldberg chose to omit the section entitled "Night," and I have followed her in these translations.

8. The Forest

Line 8: Goldberg had a little brother who died of meningitis before he was a year old.

On Poverty

Section 1—Line 2: "their secret known" (*ba'eem b'sodam*)—Cf. Genesis 49:6.

Prayers of Atonement

The Hebrew title of the poem, *Slichot,* refers to penitential prayers recited on fast days and particularly in the month of *Elul* and the first ten days of *Tishrei*, the month and days preceding Yom Kippur, the Day of Atonement. *Slichot* prayers are traditionally recited at midnight (by Ashkenazic Jews) or in the early morning hours (by Sephardic Jews), as Jewish scholars and mystics have deemed these times of the day especially favorable for experiencing the presence and closeness of God. See Shai Agnon's *Days of Awe*, where he writes: "Another reason for this practice [of reciting *Slichot* prayers at midnight] is that [then] a man's mind is composed, the body being inactive and the blood purified so that he can concentrate with his mind and heart during the last watch and achieve more than he can during the day…." (NY: Shocken 1965).

The word *slichot* is the plural of *slicha*—"pardon" or "forgiveness." In *The Collected Poems*, there are 4 sections to the poem. In Goldberg's selected poems *Early and Late*, she included only the two translated here.

Section 2—Line 2: "into the deep" (*el ha'thom*)—Cf. Genesis 1: 2: "And the earth was chaos with darkness *on the surface of the deep*" (*al penei ha'thom*).

Line 9: The phrase "all the vows"—*kol nidrei* in the Hebrew—evokes Kol Nidrei (Aramaic, "all vows"), the opening prayer of the Yom Kippur (Day of Atonement) evening service, wherein one declares the annulment of all personal vows made in the previous year. It is customary for the prayer to be repeated three times, and so poignant and popular is the prayer that the entire evening of the Day of Atonement is traditionally referred to as Kol Nidrei. The Kol Nidrei prayer dates back to at least the ninth century when it was included in the first comprehensive prayer books, *Seder Rav Amram Gaon*.

"Your lit-up window lost to the blue nights"
Line 2: For "Holy Ark," Goldberg has written "Ark of the Torah" (*aron-torah*), to rhyme with *t'horah* (pure) of line 4.
Line 6: From the reference to "your poem fell silent," it seems likely that Goldberg is addressing this poem to Avraham Ben-Yitzhak (Sonne), who published only eleven poems and then "fell silent." See the note to *On the Flowering*, p. 208.

"The world is heavy on our eyelids"
Line 2: Literally, "our head is bent."
Line 8: Literally, "the day has turned" (*hayom panah*). Cf. Jeremiah 6:4: "Alas for us, for day is declining [*ki fanah hayom*], the shadows of evening grow long." The phrase *ki fanah hayom* is repeated throughout the closing prayer service of Yom Kippur services (*Ne'ilah*), with an awareness that the day is ebbing and the metaphorical gates of life are about to be closed: "Open for us the gates, even as the gates are being locked, *for the day has turned* [*ki fanah ha'yom*]." The "pey" or

hebrew letter כ is without the dagesh—that is, pronounced as *fanah* instead of *panah*—because it follows the long vowel of *ki* (in accord with the rules of Mishnaic Hebrew).

This poem is the last one in the collection *The Green-Eyed Stalk.*

Ending

In the 1959 collection *Early and Late,* Goldberg added this poem to the poems of *From My Old Home.*

Section 1—Lines 2 & 4: For "and it was good"—*ki tov*—see Genesis 1: 3–4: "And God said, Let there be light: and there was light. And God saw the light, that *it was good*...." The *ki tov* formula ("and God saw that this [it] was [is] good") is repeated six times in the creation process. Cf. also Genesis 1:10, 12, 18, 21, 25.

Section 1—Line 3: Cf. Ecclesiasties 1:7.

Section 4—Line 8: The "ram's horn" is a reference to the *shofar,* a musical and religious instrument from biblical times. The shofar is blown in times of mourning and celebration both, and is part of the High Holiday services. Tradition has it that the blowing of the ram's horn will announce the resurrection of the dead when the Messiah comes. The ram's horn is firmly associated with the *akedah,* the binding of Isaac, when God commands that a ram be sacrificed in place of Isaac.

❧

On the Flowering (1948)

From Songs of the River

In a 1952 letter to a European literature professor named Dr. Zolai, Goldberg thanks him for choosing her poem "The River Sings to the Stone" for inclusion in a Spanish collection of Hebrew poetry. "I agree," she writes, "that these are among the best of my poems, but I am not certain whether they can be translated." This letter is quoted in Amia Leiblich's *Learning About Lea* (London: Athena Press, 2003), pp. 67–68.

The epigraph to this series is from Paul Verlaine's "Ariettes Oubliées" I. Verlaine (1844–1896) was a leader of the French Symbolist movement.

1. The River Sings to the Stone

In Hebrew, the noun *nachal* (river) is male and *even* (stone) is female; hence, the voice of the poem is in the masculine form, singing to the female stone. In the Hebrew, the poem is in rhyming couplets.
Line 9: The Hebrew contains a play on the homophonic relation between the word *ne'elam* (with an ע)—here rendered as "made mute"—and the word *ne'elam* (with an א), meaning concealed or unknown.

2. The Tree Sings to the River

In Hebrew, the noun *etz* (tree) is male; hence, the voice of the poem is in the masculine form, singing to the male river.

3. The Moon Sings to the River

In Hebrew, the noun *yare'ach* (moon) is male; hence, the voice of the poem is in the masculine, singing to the male river.

4. The Girl Sings to the River

The voice is female, singing to the male river.

5. The Blade of Grass Sings to the River

In Hebrew, the noun *giv'ol hadeshe* (blade of grass) is male. However, the noun *demut* (image)—or *demuti* (my image)—of stanzas 2 and 3 is female. Thus, the voice of the poem is female, singing to the male river. Similarly, the noun *nefesh* (the soul) of the poem's closing couplet is female.

On the Flowering

Avraham Ben Yitzhak (1883–1950), also known as Sonne, was a Hebrew poet, scholar and translator. Though his entire oeuvre consists of eleven poems, Ben Yitzhak is considered a pivotal and highly influential figure in modern Hebrew letters. Goldberg felt deep admiration and love for Ben Yitzhak, and she wrote a memoir about him entitled *Encounter with a Poet*, published shortly after his death.

In the Hebrew, this series of poems has the terzina interlocking rhyme pattern of aba, bcb, cdc, etc.

1. "The overnight flowering of the castor-oil tree"

The castor-oil tree—the *kikayon*—of the first line is traditionally known also as Jonah's Tree, the tree that God caused to spring up suddenly to shade Jonah from the relentless sun. Cf. Jonah, 4:6: "And the Lord God provided a ricinus [castor-oil] plant which grew up over Jonah, to provide shade for his head and save him from discomfort. Jonah was very happy about the plant." However, as suddenly as the plant grew, so did it wither away, leaving him unprotected from the heat of the sun. Cf. also Jonah 4: 7–11.

The poet is playing on the word similarity between the final word in line 8—*d'mee* (silence)—and the final word of the poem—*damee* (my blood).

2. "Old woman, sun-burnt and blue-eyed."

Line 3: For *hahevel*—here rendered as breath, but meaning also vanity—Cf. Ecclesiastics 1: 2: "Vanity of vanities; all is vanity."

4. "This firmament—straight and wide-edged"

Line 10: Cf. Job 21: 33: "The clods of the valley shall be sweet unto him." Also Job 38: 37–38: "Who can number the clouds in wisdom? Or who can stay the bottles of heaven, when the dust groweth into hardness, and the clods cleave fast together?"

5. "How trains passed by! Silvered tracks"

Line 2: The word *kisuf*—"silvered" or "silvering"—also means "longing." The poet is evoking both meanings; hence my rendering of the tracks humming as "long and longing."

Line 6: Literally, "shadows of branches, electricity and fears." The word *khashmal* (electricity, in modern Hebrew) appears once in the Bible, in Ezekiel 1:4: "And I looked, and, lo, a stormy wind came sweeping out of the north—a huge cloud and flashing fire, surrounded by a radiance; and in the center of it, in the center of the fire, *a gleam as of amber* [*k'ein ha'khasmal*]." The exact meaning of the term *khasmal*, translated in this verse as "a gleam of amber," is uncertain.

7. "To the solitary of the night"

Line 3: In the phrase *shalvat yichud*—here rendered as "the quietude of union"—Goldberg may be alluding to the Kabbalistic meaning of *yichud* (union or convergence). In the Kabbalah, the world is divided into different realms, *Sefirot*, defined by their closeness to and awareness of God. The tenth and last *Sefirah*, the *Sefirah of Malchut* (Kingdom), more commonly referred to as the *Shechinah*, is the feminine aspect of God and the manifestation of God's love and compassion. According to the Kabbalah, the "task" of the Jewish people is to bring about a union (a *yichud*) of the *Shechinah* and the other nine "masculine" *Sefirot*.

The mystical merging of the Shechinah and the other nine *Sefirot* is reflected in, and even facilitated by, the union of man and woman. Indeed, immediately following the wedding ritual under the bridal canopy (the *chuppah*), the bride and groom go off to a separate room where they can be alone together, for the first time. This phase in the wedding ceremony is also called *yichud* and is considered a sanctification of the convergence of two souls, and the convergence of the spiritual and the sensual.

9. "One abandoned star in the wild dark"

Line 10: Literally, "the eternal spring bloomed, bloomed." However, for the line's rhythm and to echo the two-syllable Hebrew (*henetz, henetz*), I have put the verb into the present perfect form. The verb form evokes the well-known verse from the love poetry of Song of Songs: "I went down to the nut grove to see the budding of the vale;

to see if the vines had blossomed, the *pomegranates had bloomed* [*henetzu rimonim*]" (6:11).

Goldberg has established a sound link between these closing four lines of the poem through their opening words: *henetz* of line 10 ("will bloom") echoes *nitsotz* of line 8 ("spark") which echoes *nitzan* of line 7 ("bud").

from Love Sonnets
The note regarding the thirteen-line form of these sonnets is Goldberg's. There are eight sonnets in this series—four are translated here.

3. "Today I remember your boyhood"
Line 4: For "[o]nly your mother's image *withdraws, and is gone*" (*khomekek v'overet*), Cf. Song of Songs 5:6: "I opened to my beloved, but my beloved had withdrawn and is gone…"

4. "An aged moon adorned in the heat-wave's halo"
Line 9: For "like a driven leaf"—Cf. Job 13:25.

7. "A sudden shower at the edge of April"
Line 13: For "and it is good" (*ki tov*), see the note for **Ending** in *Early Poems*, p. 206.

The Lament of Odysseus
See Homer's *The Odyssey*, Book xi and Samuel 2, 1:19–27—King David's heart-wrenching lament for Saul and his son Jonathan, David's beloved friend and comrade, both slain in battle.

In an interview, Goldberg discussed this text in the following terms: "This poem was written during wartime and I wanted to express in it the meeting with the dead, the meeting of one person who carries in his heart guilt for staying alive…. Not by chance I used the style of [David's] lament…—one of the Bible's most disturbing lyrical outcries" (Galia Yardeni, *16 Conversations with Writers*, as quoted by Tuvia Ruebner in his monograph *Lea Goldberg* [Tel Aviv: Sifriat Poalim, 1980] p. 217). In an earlier 1939 article about the role of poetry in war-time, Goldberg mentions David's lament as "…the first, or one of the first, pacifist songs in the world" (Ruebner, 71). Note: Ruebner's text is in Hebrew; translations into English from his text are my own.

Lines 5, 12, 20: "How the mighty have fallen"—Cf. Samuel 2, 1: 25–27: "How the mighty have fallen in the thick of battle—Jonathan, slain on your heights! I grieve for you, my brother Jonathan. You were most dear to me. Your love was wonderful to me more than the love of women. How the mighty have fallen!"
Line 10: For "eyes blinded"—*einayim kamot*—Cf. Kings 1, 14:4.
Line 16: Cf. Psalms 124:4: "Our soul is escaped as a bird out of the snare…; the snare is broken, and we have fled." See also *The Odyssey* Book x, where Odysseus and his men break free of Circe's trap.
Lines 17, 18: "Cain's mark"—Cf. Genesis 4:15.

From the Book of the Dead

The term "The Book of the Dead"—*sefer hameitim*—appears in only one place in the Jewish sources, in the Talmud, Tractate *Rosh Hashanah* 32b. It is coupled there with the more widely referenced *sefer hachayim*—"The Book of the Living" (or "The Book of Life").

Within the context of the poem, Goldberg may be referring to the Egyptian Book of the Dead. This sacred text from ancient Egypt of approximately 1600 B.C. was a collection of funerary chapters of spells, formulas and passwords. The text was intended to be read by the deceased during their journey into the underworld. It enabled the dead to overcome obstacles of the underworld and not lose their way.

Section 2: The seven days and seven nights refer to *shiv'ah* (literally "seven")—Judaism's traditional week of mourning wherein the mourner stops all activity to devote him/herself wholly to remembering the departed one and to the mourning process.

"And will they ever come, days of forgiveness and grace"

Goldberg's biographer and literary executor Tuvia Ruebner states that this poem is Goldberg's response to a literary debate that was raging in Palestine during World War II, regarding the legitimacy of lyrical poems. According to Ruebner, poets such as Natan Alterman argued that in a time of war, the poet must write war songs, "mobilized poetry," whereas Goldberg argued that even in war times, the poet still has the right—even the obligation—to write poems of nature and love. In this poem Goldberg poses the question of whether the poet may be a "simple wanderer" in the fields, even as these fields are "stiffened with blood and terror"—and the quiet, certain answer of renewal is delivered in the Whitmanesque final line. See Ruebner's *Lea Goldberg* (Sifriyat Poalim and Kibbutz HaMeuchad Press, 1980) pp. 69–74, 116.

The addressed "you" of the poem is in the female form (*at*).

Elul in the Galilee

Elul is the last month in the Jewish calendar, usually falling between mid-August and mid-September. This is the month preceding the Jewish Days of Awe—Rosh Hashanah (the New Year) and Yom Kippur (the Day of Atonement). During the month of *Elul,* the individual is enjoined to ponder the past year, make amends and prepare the self for the introspection and solemnity of the Day of Atonement.

Section 1—Line 9: For "And it was evening"—*vayehee erev*—Cf. Genesis 1:5: "God called the light Day, and the darkness he called Night, And it was evening and it was morning, the first day." The refrain "and it was evening..." is repeated at the end of the descriptions of all six days of creation.

Section 2—Line 1: "Remember me kindly," literally "Remember me for good," (*zichroonee li'tovah*) evokes the High Holiday liturgy: *zochreinu l'chayim melech chofetz b'chaim u'katveynu b'sefer hachayim* ("Remember us for life, O King Who desires life, and inscribe us in the Book of Life"). However, while the address in the prayer is a communal one to a singular God (*zochreinu*), in the poem the speaker is singular, addressing a plural you *(zichroonee)*.

In the Jerusalem Hills

Section 4: The opening word of this section, repeated in the section's penultimate line—*eicha*—is an elevated and elegiac form of "how." The word *eicha* also evokes the Book of Lamentations (called *eicha* in Hebrew, for the book's opening word)—a book lamenting the destruction of the First Temple and of Jerusalem, and commemorating the resulting suffering of exile and dislocation.

❧

Lightning in the Morning (1955)

The relationship between "lightning" and "morning" is accentuated in the Hebrew through the identical letters, in different order, of the two words: *bet, resh, kof* in *barak* (lightning) and *bet, kof, resh* in *boker* (morning).

The Broken Vessel

In the original 1955 collection *Lightning in the Morning*, Goldberg had three sections to this poem. In the selected poems of *Early and Late* (1959/2003), Goldberg omitted the first section, and included only the two sections translated here.

The Hebrew idiom "like a broken vessel" (*k'kheres hanishbar*) means something worthless or useless.
Section 1—Line 4: Literally, "they'll wrap him in a prayer shawl of blue." The idiom "a prayer shawl of all blue" (*tallit shekulah tekhelet*) originates in Midrash Rabbah, Bamidbar Rabbah, Parsha 18:3 in a Talmudic discussion of the rebellious biblical figure of Korach. The phrase means "a paragon of virtue" and connotes false piety.
Section 2—Line 6: Cf. Samuel 2, 1:19: "The beauty of Israel is slain

upon your high places: how are the mighty fallen!", and Samuel 2, 1:25: "O Jonathan, slain on your high places!" The verses are taken from David's lament for Saul and his son Jonathan.

April *Khamsin*

Khamsin is a heat wave, characterized by a hot westerly wind coming from the Sahara. The word origin is from the Arabic for fifty (*khamsūn*, from *khams*, five), so called because the wind is said to blow fifty days each year, from April till June.

Line 12: Literally, "and every scent and stir was *bone of my self*" (*etsem me'atsmi*). The root letters in Hebrew of "bone" and "self" are the same. The phrase "bone of my self" echoes the biblical verse "bone of my bones" (*etsem me'atsamai*")—Cf. Genesis 2:23: "Then Man said: This one is bone of my bones and flesh of my flesh. This one shall be called Woman, for from Man was she taken."

Trees
1. Pine
While there are some wild pine woodlands in Israel, the vast majority of the pine forests are cultivated ones, transplanted from other regions.

2. Eucalyptus
Line 3: The Hebrew for "my rock, my savior"—*tsuri, yeshuati*—evokes the popular Hanukkah song *Maoz Tzur Yeshuati* ("Mighty Rock of My Salvation"). This song, addressed to God, is thought to have originated in Germany in the 13th century. It is traditionally sung by Ashkenazic Jews after the lighting of the Hanukkah lights. In his notes to Goldberg's *Selected Poems* (Sifriat Poalim, 1970), Ruebner suggests that the reference to Hanukkah is to evoke the notion of revival after destruction.

3. The Castor-Oil Plant (Jonah's Tree)
See note for **On the Flowering**—section 1: "The overnight flowering of the castor-oil tree" p. 208.

Coat of Many Colors

The reference in the title and the poem is to Joseph, the coat of many colors his father Jacob made for him, and the great enmity of Joseph's brothers toward him. Cf. Genesis 37: 3–5, 19–35.

Poems of the Journey's End

Section 2—Line 4: Cf. Ecclesiastics 1:9: "The thing that hath been, it is that which shall be; and that which is done is that which shall be done; and there is no new thing under the sun. The "you" in this section is in the masculine form *atah*.

Section 3—Line 5: This line evokes the phrase that opens the *Amidah* prayers—the core prayer of the morning service: "My God, open my lips so they may declare thy praise." This phrase (and the entire Amidah) service is spoken silently. The phrase originates in Psalms 51:17.
Line 6: Cf. Lamentations 5:21: "O Lord…renew our days as of old."
Line 8: Literally, "lest my day be for me habit."

The Love of Teresa De Meun

The opening note to this series is Goldberg's. In the original *Lightning in the Morning* collection, the note appears at the end of the book. In *Early and Late* selected poems, Goldberg moved the note to the significantly more prominent placement at the series' beginning.

Tuvia Ruebner notes that the choice to use the Petrarchan sonnet form for this series of twelve sonnets may have been influenced by Goldberg's own translations into Hebrew of twenty two of Petrarch's sonnets, published in 1953. See Ruebner's *Lea Goldberg*, p. 127.

1. "This unrelenting curse with which I am cursed"
Line 2: Literally, "I have nourished and brought up the wisdom of years." With the phrase "nurtured and brought up" (*romamti v'gidalti*), Goldberg is quoting and reversing one of the opening verses from Isaiah, spoken by God: "I have nourished and brought up (*gidalti v'romamti*) children and they have rebelled against me" (1:2).

3. "And were you to banish me to the desert"
The reference is to Abraham's banishment of his handmaiden Hagar and their son Ishmael to the desert (at his wife Sarah's bidding). Cf. Genesis 21: 9–21.

7. "Long hours, little moments too":
Lines 9–11: Cf. Joshua 10:12–15: "On that occasion, when the Lord routed the Amorites before the Israelites, Joshua addressed the Lord; he said in the presence of the Israelites: 'Stand still, O sun, at Givon; O moon, in the Valley of Ayalon!' And the sun stood still, and the moon halted, while a nation wreaked judgment on its foes—as is written in the Book of Jashar. Thus the sun halted in mid-heaven, and did not press on to set, for a whole day; for the Lord fought for Israel. Neither before nor since has there ever been such a day, when the Lord acted on words spoken by a man."
Line 9: Cf. Joshua 2:11—"…and there was no spirit [courage] left in any person before you…"

10. "Oh, how beautiful was the city that day":
Lines 7–8: Cf. Psalms 114:4, 6.

You Are Wondrous
The poem's title, "You Are Wondrous" (*niflahtah*), repeated in section one, echoes David's lament for his beloved Jonathan. Cf. Samuel 2: 1–26. The "you" is in the male form.

From the Songs of My Beloved Land
The title of the poem, *me'shirei eretz ahavati,* means literally "From the Songs of the Land of My Love." In the Hebrew, the word *ahavati* ("my love") may be read as multiple in meaning, referring back to the aforementioned land, an individual and a concept too. In order to preserve the lyrical nature of the Hebrew title, I have translated it as "From the Songs of My Beloved Land." In order to convey the multiple meanings embedded in the title, I have translated "*eretz ahavati*" when repeated in section 2 (lines 1 and 6) in two different ways.

Section 1—Lines 1 & 11: Literally, "my motherland, poor ornamental land." Goldberg's neologistic collocation "ornamental land" (*eretz noi*) alludes to the phrase *atsei-noi*—ornamental trees, non-fruit-bearing trees. For "motherland," Goldberg uses an elevated and less commonly used word—*mechora* (place of origins). Cf. Ezekiel 15:3 and 29:14.

Section 2—Line 16: Cf. Song of Songs, 5:2: "I sleep but my heart wakes: it is the voice of my beloved that knocks saying, Open to me, my sister, my love…"

ॐ

Last Words (1959)

From the Songs of Zion
1. Night
Lines 3–4: Cf. Psalms 137: 1–4—"By the rivers of Babylon, there we sat down, when we remembered Zion…and our captors asked us there for songs, saying, 'Sing for us from the songs of Zion.' But how shall we sing the Lord's song in a strange land?" Line 3 and the first half of line 4 in Goldberg's poem are exact quotations from these verses.

2. The Quarry
Stone (*even*) in Hebrew is female. Hence, in place of the non-gendered pronoun "it," the literal rendering of the text would be: "the stone in *her* refusal / …the secret of *her* heart / …" etc. The "your" of "your hand" (line 5) is male.

4. Migrating Birds
Line 5: "the Traveler's prayer," *tefillat haderech*, is a reference to a prayer Jews traditionally recite at the beginning of a journey. In the prayer, the traveler asks for a safe passage to her destination.
Line 9: For "deep waters" (*t'hom*), Cf. Genesis 1:2.

Three Days

Section 2: This entire section seems to be in dialogue with Song of Songs—in particular lines 3, 9, 15, which echo Song of Songs 5:2 ("...the voice of my beloved knocks, saying, Open to me, my sister, my love..."). In Goldberg's poem, the commands "Answer me" and "Open for me" are addressed to a man.

Section 2—Line 18: Cf. Song of Songs 5: 7: "The watchmen who went about the city found me, they smote me, they wounded me; the watchers of the walls took my veil away from me."

The Lovers on the Beach

Section 1—Lines 8, 16, 27: The refrain of "Come to me, my bride" (*bo'ee kallah*)—which comes here at the close of each stanza—is taken from the popular Sabbath song "Lecha Dodi," sung at Friday night prayers. The origin of this phrase is from the Talmud (Sabbath Tractate, 119a), where the Sabbath itself is described as the beautiful and long-awaited bride.

From My Mother's House

Section 1—Line 16: The reference is to the wig that some religious Jewish women wear after they marry.

Illuminations

The Rimbaudesque title is in English in the original.
Section 1: The addressed "you" of this section is male.

Section 3: The addressed "you" of the first line is female. The three angels evoke the three angel-messengers who visited Abraham, to tell him that his barren wife Sara would bear a child. Cf. Genesis 18: 1–16.

❧

With this Night (1964)

In a letter to a friend, Goldberg wrote the following regarding this collection: "What you say about my last book—true, I know it doesn't ravish the heart. Even sadness is more charming, gentle and soothing in young than elderly people. My poems are very much like the thorns around Jerusalem, and I love dryness….I hesitated whether to publish this book, but I did it to prove to myself that I'm still writing" (quoted in *Learning About Lea*, p. 304). This was the last poetry collection published in Goldberg's lifetime.

The Shortest Journey

1. Tel Aviv 1935
Final line: In his notes to Goldberg's *Selected Poems* (Sifriat Poalim, 1970), Tuvia Ruebner suggests that the poem's final image is an allusion to the midrash whereby, in the Messianic age, all the worlds' churches will gather in Israel.

2. Evening in a Café
Line 1: The allusion is to Joseph's coat of many colors. Cf. Genesis 37: 3, 24, 31–32.
Line 12: In the original collection of *With this Night*, Goldberg wrote this line as "in a *secret pact* [*brit setarim*] with my clock"; in the selected poetry of *Early and Late*, the line was revised to read "in an *autumnal pact* [*brit stavit*] with my clock."

3. A Rainy Autumn Night and a Clear Morning
Line 12: "are hers—": in Hebrew "city" (*ir*) is gendered female.
Line 16: This line is an allusion to and reversal of Song of Songs 1:5: "I am black but comely."

4. Then She Had
The "she" of the title and the poem is the city. See previous note.

5. I Walked Then
Line 10: The word Goldberg uses here for silence—*dumah*—is also
a name given to the guardian angel of the dead.

A Nameless Journey
Uncharacteristically, Goldberg ends this poem with the date and
place of composition. In the original, the date is in its Hebrew form:
Elul, Tashach. For *Elul,* see the note to **Elul in the Galilee**, in *On the
Flowering,* (p. 212).

Passed to Another World
Section 1—Lines 3–4: Literally, "but my heart is wasted / by hun-
ger"—*m'zeh ra'av.* Cf. Moses' farewell song to the people of Israel in
Deuteronomy 32:24.

Section 3—Line 12: "The Book of your Kingdom"—*sefer malchut'cha*—
may be an allusion to the tenth divine emanation, *malchut,* as num-
bered and explained in *Sefer Yetzirah* ("The Book of Formation"), the
classic text of Kabbalah (Jewish mysticism).

Section 4—Line 6: For "The Book of the Dead" (*sefer hameitim*),
see note to **From the Book of the Dead**, in *On the Flowering,* p. 211.
Sefer hameitim functions here also as a reversal of the traditional *sefer
hachayim,* the Book of Life (or, the Book of the Living), in which
believing Jews pray to be inscribed.

God Once Commanded Us
Line 1–2: The Tree of Life is one of the two trees in the Garden of
Eden whose fruit is forbidden to Adam and Eve. Adam and Eve eat
of the Tree of Knowledge, but God banishes them from the garden
before they can eat of the Tree of Life and gain immortality. Cf.
Genesis 2: 22, 24.
Line 11: "And it is good"—*v'zeh tov* (literally "and this is good")—
echoes "and it is good"—*ki tov*—from the creation story. Cf. Genesis
1: 3–4, 10, 12, 18, 21, 25.

Line 12: "the blade of cutting cold" (*lahav hakor hachotech*) may be Goldberg's reversal of "the flame of the ever-turning sword" (*lahat hacherev hamithapechet*) placed by God at the eastern edge of the Garden of Eden to guard the way to the Tree of Life. Cf. Genesis 3:24.

Portrait of the Poet as an Old Man

In section one, the first-person voice of the poem is in the male form. In sections 2 and 3 of the poem, the addressed "you" is in the male form.

Far Away

Section 1—Line 13: Literally, "the explicit name"—*hashem hameforash*—a reference to God's ineffable name, the Tetragrammaton, signified by the Hebrew letters yod, heh, vav, heh (YHWH).

₰

The Remains of Life (1978)

This collection was published posthumously. While a few of the poems in this volume were first published in journals, most of them were found in Goldberg's notebooks after her death. Tuvia Ruebner, who prepared this volume for publication, states in his end-note: "There is no knowing whether Lea Goldberg would have included all the poems she typed up were she still alive.... And she, who aspired toward a degree of perfection...would have undoubtedly omitted the poetic pieces I have collected here under the name 'Fragments'. I bring them in her memory."

Ruebner included 59 poems, or poetic fragments, in the collection—the number of years Goldberg lived. Unfortunately, two poems that were not the poet's, but were found amongst her papers, were erroneously included in the book. These two poems were included under the title "Fragments," on pages 13 and 14 in the original collection.

"And the poem I did not write"
Line 10: Goldberg utilizes here the traditional epic evocation of the Muse. See, for example, the opening verse of Homer's *The Odyssey*.

Jerusalem, Earthly and Heavenly
The concept *Yerushalyim shel mata ve'shel ma'lah* ("Jerusalem, Earthly and Heavenly"—literally "Jerusalem of below and of above") conveys the rabbinic belief that Jerusalem was built in two parallel spheres: the spiritual realm (heavenly Jerusalem) and the physical realm (earthly Jerusalem). The term itself originates in the Babylonian Talmud, *Ta'anit* 5a. In an exchange between two rabbis, one says to the other that "The Holy One, blessed be He, proclaimed: 'I will not come into the upper Jerusalem (*yerushalayim shel ma'alah*) until I enter the lower Jerusalem (*yerushalayim shel mata*).'" Thus God himself is in exile until his people are redeemed.

Section 2—Lines 8–9: "David, King of Israel / lives forever" is a popular Hebrew song originating in a passage from Talmud, *Rosh Hashanah* Tractate 25a.

Section 3—Line 12: The reference is to the Palestinian city of Hebron, famous for its glass blowers. The royal blue glass produced in the city is its best known product.

"The day turned."
For the repeated phrase "the day turned" (*hayom panah*), see note to "The world is heavy on our eyelids" in *Early Poems*, p. 205.

"My entire life summed up in that one moment—"
In the Hebrew, line 2 reads *keren shel or al keren hatzvi*. The word *keren* means both "ray" and "antler" (or "horn").

"There were questions"
Line 7: The "her" refers to the land of line 5, gendered female in Hebrew.

from Small Poems
3. All of Night's Stars
Line 2: Cf. Psalm 115: 15: "The heavens belong to God, but the earth He gave over to mankind." This phrase is incorporated into the *Hallel* service (prayers of praise), spoken during morning prayers at the beginning of a new month and on other festival days.

On the Dangers of Smoking
Line 7: Literally, "Silence is wisdom's fence"—Cf. Sayings of the Fathers 3:13 and Proverbs 10: 19.

The Remains of Life
The title "The Remains of Life"—*sh'ayreet hakhayim*—is reminiscent of two other Hebrew phrases: *sh'ayreet haplita* ("remaining survivors," used specifically to refer to Holocaust survivors), and *acharit hayamim* (the End of Days, the apocalypse).
Section 2: the addressee is female.

Sickness
Final line: For *pnei t'hom*, Cf. Genesis 1, 2: "And darkness was upon the face of the depths."

White Poplar Leaves
Section 1—Lines 3–4: Goldberg has used a non-grammatical formulation by transforming the verb *shotek* or *shotkim*—"keeping quiet"—into a transitive verb, with the direct object being "the evening hours" of the following line. I have tried to recreate some of the original dissonance of these two lines in my rendering.
Line 5: The addressee is female.

Section 2: The repeated "the name"—*hashem*—is another title for God.

Section 3—Line 1 *&* 3: Literally, "Peace unto me."

"Tomorrow I will die" and "This will be the judgment"

These two poems—Goldberg's last—were written in the hospital, a few days before her death. The "you" in "Tomorrow I will die" is plural.

"This will be the judgment"

Line 16: The word for "the living"—*hakhayim*—means also "life."

᙮

Uncollected Poems

Khamsin

For title, see note for **April *Khamsin*** from *Lightning in Morning* p. 214.

Line 3: *seder* is the Passover meal. The Hebrew word for "Marranos"—*anusim*—means those who are compelled or forced to do something. The Marranos were the Jews of Spain and Portugal who were forced to convert but continued to practice their religion in secret.

Ne'ilah / Closing

The title refers to the concluding prayer on Yom Kippur (the Day of Atonement). *Ne'ilah* literally means "closing" and refers to the symbolic closing of the gates of heaven (*Ne'ilat Shearim*). Throughout this service, the word *katveinu* ("**inscribe** us [in the Book of Life]"), employed from Rosh Hashanah in all services up to Ne'ilah, is replaced with *khatmeinu* ("**seal** us [in the Book of Life]"); indeed, the entire service—prayed as the sun is setting—is marked by a sense of ending and an accompanying urgency. This series of poems is marked by an abundance of motifs from the Ne'ilah service.

1. The Sun Will Turn

Stanza 2, Line 1: "each other"—*zo b'zo*—is female to female. In Hebrew the sun is gendered both male and female.

2. Because the Day Fades
Literally, "Because the Day Turns" (*ki panah yom*). See note to "The world is heavy on our eyelids" in *Early Poems*, p. 205.

3. Open for Us a Gate
The reference is to the metaphorical Gates of Life, through which the Jew seeks to pass before the end of prayers and the sealing of the Gate.

4. *Ne'ilah*
Line 2: In traditional synagogues, men and women sit separately. The women's section is often located upstairs, where the women are meant to be unseen and unheard.

Index of First Lines

A basket full of stars 58

A hundred silences and not one tear. 77

A landscape like this has no answers. .167

A rainy morning. Don't get up. Don't smoke, don't 184

A restless blossoming in the darkness of our garden 65

A sudden shower at the edge of April. 72

A young poet suddenly falls silent 163

Above my house. 169

All of night's large stars remain there .176

All the riddles time has posed. 87

All the shutters in my room are closed 197

All things which are 79

Already the silences are easy 166

An aged moon adorned with the heat-wave's halo 71

And beyond the land of the living 74

And if ever I am asked to say 92

And if I forget the prayer? 115

And it will bear so easily. 58

And so you go out into the streets 128

And the poem I did not write 164

And this will be the judgment 191

And tomorrow again the throat's suffocation 197

And were you to banish me to the desert 99
And will they ever come, days of forgiveness and grace 76
And you walked among the dead 151
Another measure of distance. Another tomorrow and another . . 177
Apples like these, my mother says 124
At night the boxcars passed by. I didn't raise my eyes 176
At night when I closed my eyes I saw a leaf 48
At the Holy Gate 152
At the moment it was decreed I shouldn't wait 180
Because they were crimson the paths that wandered toward
sunset 34
Break your bread in two 168
But it was a wondrous spring 179
By law I am not entitled 106
Carry your dream to the stars of the Nile 46
Cherry-resin—sweet and transparent 41
Dead earth and a living sky 148
Deep within the mirror it lives 88
Desire nothing 158
Did a golden bell chime in the high heavens? 113
Don't try to follow the new generation 154
During the day I never cried. And 199
Even this landscape 156
Even to little ones like me 57
Far away 156
Far away 157
Farewell to me, farewell 189
For one who does not believe 149
For three days his memory would not leave me 120
From my window and from yours 102
God once commanded us to stand strong and steadfast 153
Have you seen the rain? We are quiet 129
Here autumn is the border of spring 147
Here heavy birds alight to rest 86
Here I cannot hear the voice of the cuckoo 91
How can one lone bird 81

How can we bring our dying heart. 67

How could a blithe bird stray. 80

How the passing of Time tries me 95

How the trains passed by! Silvered tracks. 64

I am cold to my bones. The landscape before me. 117

I am green and replete like a song that has passed through

the grass. 140

I am not in the desert. There is a clock here. 176

I am the one on high 55

I cried out: "Answer me!". 119

I imagined that time had stood still 49

I kissed the stone in the chill of her dream. 53

I left and never returned. 48

I lie like a stone among these hills 78

I never loved a city. 26

I pass by like this pain 146

I picked a wildflower and tossed it away. I waited 176

I saw a body stripped bare 93

I saw my God in the café. 29

I sit at my desk. 154

I stand in the heart of the desert 119

I strode into this night. 185

I waited seven days for a tear to fall .75

I walked then. 138

I walked with the boats and I stood with the bridges. 143

I was never taught how to stand in prayer 201

I'll rise, I will rise 183

If not for the wind we could hear. 125

In everything there is at least an eighth part. 165

In streets such as these live the simplest folk 36

In the land of my love the almond tree blossoms. 109

In the lit-up window square. 144

In the poor land that I love 110

In the purified silence. 188

Into a dark and sealed night. 136

Into this quiet the voice 49

It is not the sea that stands between us 157
It isn't necessary 26
It was understood as pretend, all pretend, Perrault's tales 39
It was wrenched from its roots, its core 125
It's been weeks since anyone has addressed me 142
Land of low winds, I was yours 141
Last climb in the bronze hills 174
Lightning and dawn. Light struck light 85
Like stars that find their way to every window 33
Like the light ray that passes through 95
Long hours, little moments too 100
My days are engraved in my poems 25
My entire life summed up in that one moment 172
My hands are pale 196
My mother's mother died 123
My motherland, beautiful and poor 108
My room is so small 142
My snow was light-blue 175
Night passed me by 59
O let me die with my eyes wide open 42
Of all your forgotten ones I 182
Oh, how beautiful was the city that day 103
Old woman, sun-burnt and blue-eyed 61
Once again distances…and the blood of falling leaves 32
Once upon a time in the high skies 38
One abandoned star in the wild dark 68
One after another things 200
Only one step 166
Only the hills are already awake 150
Our days are quiet like the child's slumber 42
Our loves are not many 174
Over one of the hills 129
People are walking in the pretend city 168
Pine needles. Their gold dark and warm 40
Remember me kindly in such an autumn 77

Sated with wandering, old Odysseus descended to the
Underworld 73
She was a golden leaf falling in the sunlight. 144
Simply 25
Snow fell 186
Somewhere something somebody there 146
Stubborn, deaf, mute 113
Teach me, my God, to bless and pray. 97
Ten times 185
Ten years after your death 152
That death would rise up in his window. 62
That same spring morning 114
The city in a many-colored robe. 135
The clasp of sand and stone 170
The crescent moon is draped in black. 107
The cruel dawn. 89
The curls on my head silver in the moonlight. 95
The day turned. 171
The green today is very green 127
The hills today are shadows of hills. 178
The ivy that climbed the dark walls of the hut 35
The month divined over chamomile leaves. 43
The one who bore my golden autumn 54
The overnight flowering of the castor-oil tree 60
The pain. 118
The path is so lovely—said the boy. 96
"The remains of life," he said. 185
The shortest journey is the one across years 139
The stars are very beautiful. 58
The strands of rain like violin strings 101
The winds hide in the folds of the curtains. 37
The wise men will testify that the sun. 126
The world is heavy on our eyelids. 47
The world still stands its ground. 187
The years have made up my face. 159

Then she still had the scent of sea 137
Then the aerials on the city's roofs were 134
There are many like me: lonely and sad 30
There were questions 173
They don't want to remember the truth 89
They withstood the heat wave 113
They've passed to another world 151
This firmament—straight and wide-edged 63
This unrelenting curse with which I am cursed 98
Thorns. Rocks. Thistles. I walked 148
Those who knew me will remember 195
To the solitary of the night: the storm has died 66
Today I remember your boyhood 70
Today the gardeners are sad 126
Tomorrow I will die 190
We are dreamers. Don't fool 94
We were very young 186
We were young without hope 186
What will our end be? Night's omens 118
What will our end be? The skies 117
What will our end be? 118
What will remain? Words, words like the ash 104
Where am I? How can I explain where I am? 142
Where will the current carry my small face? 56
White poplar leaves 188
Why don't you stop, fool 154
Windmill, windmill 140
With this night and all its silences 133
Yes, I have more 181
Yes, I know this is a peerless day 90
You are wondrous, wholly wondrous .105
You ask for nothing 149
You came to me to open my eyes 43
You said: Day chases day and night—night 96
You sent the owl 122
You tell me that this fire 115

You were for me blessed earth 69
Your honey? Who will remember your honey? 145
Your lit-up window lost to the blue nights 45
Your nearness and the sea's 121
Your portrait is so peaceful. You are other 31

Part II:
Drama

Lady of the Castle

Matti Megged

Introduction

The play *Lady of the Castle*, which appears here in translation, belongs, at first sight, to that category of plays on "actual" themes which constituted the largest part of the original plays performed on Israeli stages during the first decade after the establishment of the State. This play too—which was produced at the Cameri Theater in 1956—turns on a known and specific historical matter, from the near and familiar past: the saving of Jewish children from the different places of refuge where they had hidden or been hidden by non-Jews during the Nazi regime in Europe, in those cases where the benefactors had no intention of returning the children to their people. Many Israelis were sent, or volunteered, to discover these forced child converts in their various hiding-places, to release them and bring them to the land of Israel; many more Israelis knew of such incidents more personally, with members of their own families, or close friends, involved in them one way or another. Thus the topical and historical background of the play was familiar to its spectators; and the characters in it—two emissaries from Israel, on the one hand, and a Jewish girl who had been hidden by her non-Jewish benefactor (in this case, Count Zabrodsky), on the other, fulfilled the unwritten requirements placed at the time on plays belonging to this category. So too with the plot of the play, which concludes with the anticipated rescue of the Jewish girl and hints at her imminent migration to the land of Israel, like the many thousands whose lot this was in reality.

Yet in truth this play is far different in its essence from all the other topical plays of its time. The fact is that in spite of its historical background, characters and plot, which it shares with such plays, it is not in these things that the essential nature and uniqueness of this play is to be found. The actual historical matter mentioned above was no more than a point-of-departure around which the poet Lea Goldberg, author of this play, tried to weave an exceptional, even extraordinary, poetic-dramatic pageant, which has almost nothing at all to do with the topical subject-matter itself.

The real, inner conflict of this play is *not* of course the visible conflict between the emissaries from Israel and Lena, the girl who has been hidden in the castle, or the Count, its former owner—nor is its significance limited to the events that happen to these people on the one night during which the plot occurs. The essence of the conflict is in the uncompromising contrast between two different spiritual-intellectual worlds. On the one hand stands the moribund world which has been condemned to death, with its treasures, charms and noble though sickly and delusory isolation, a world which, when the plot occurs, is no longer anything but an abode of ghosts, though it still retains some of its past fascination. On the other hand is the world of the bright present, a materialistic world, focused around the primary and simple concerns of life, work, and food for *all* its inhabitants and not only for the select few, a world which gazes with justified suspicion upon all the ghost castles with their guards and fascinations.

Even though this play is written in "prosaic" language, in the idiom and concepts of its specific time and place, it is apparent that it has been written by a *poet*, one who cannot—and perhaps she does not even try to—hide either her secret yearnings for the magic of the moribund world, which is symbolized here by the castle and is represented by its owner, or her deep sorrow over the inevitable death of this world. Even the strands from which the characters of the Count and Lena are woven, their delusions and their bitter dialogue, are the work of a true poet. Anyone familiar with the poems and stories of Lea Goldberg will certainly recognize a number of strands of her poetic world, which have been woven into the tapestry of this play.

But it is just as apparent that the play has been written by a *Hebrew* poet, a Jewish writer, who cannot and will not allow herself to be seduced by the alien and diseased charms of this "castle," with its legends and its ghosts, and thus finally takes a clear stand on the side of the representatives of the "present," who by rescuing the Jewish girl from the prison of this castle, actually give a hand to its complete liquidation.

It seems, indeed, that because of this very conflict between the two worlds—which takes place also within the poet herself—Goldberg displays a kind of hesitancy or slackness, both in her representation of the world of the "past" and in her justification of the "present" world. It is possible that her moral sense—her human, Jewish sense—does not allow her to express fully and to the limits of her poetic powers the yearning she has for the fascinations of the "castle"; concomitantly, her loyalty to her poetic world does not allow her to give full voice to the argument—which she too considers as just—of the representatives of the "present" or the "future" against everything that the castle symbolizes.

At the same time there is no doubt that *Lady of the Castle* is distinguished by one important quality which is not to be found in most of the other plays (Israeli and perhaps not only Israeli) which deal with topical subjects, and this is its attempt to raise the immediate and familiar subject to another level, to add another dimension to it; one which is simultaneously very universal and very personal.

(Note: Lea Goldberg's oeuvre includes three plays—*Sea in the Window*, *Lady of the Castle* and *The Mute Mountain*. However, *Lady of the Castle* was her only play ever published and produced. Upon its premier in 1956 at the Tel Aviv Cameri Theater, the play was received with positive reviews, and subsequently was translated into a variety of other languages, including French, English and Japanese. The play was produced and performed in various places around the world, including Tokyo, London, Berlin and New York. *Lady of the Castle* also served as the inspiration for an English language ballad-opera of the same name, which was later reworked into German and performed in a 50th anniversary commemoration of the end of World War II. The play remains topical, as evidenced by its spring 2005 production at the International Theater of Chicago.)

    —updated by Rachel Tzvia Back, December 2004.

Lady of the Castle

A Dramatic Episode in Three Acts

TRANSLATED FROM THE HEBREW
by T. Carmi

First published in 1974 by the Institute for the Translation of Hebrew
Literature Ltd., in cooperation with the Cultural Division of the
Department for Education and Culture in the Diaspora, w.z.o.
© All translation rights reserved by the Institute for
the Translation of Hebrew Literature Ltd., 1974.
Copyright © of this English version by T. Carmi.

All performing rights of this play are fully protected, and permission
to perform it must be obtained in advance from ACUM, 120 Roth-
schild Blvd., Tel Aviv.

CHARACTERS

MICHAEL SAND	a librarian from Palestine, about 40 years old.
DR. DORA RINGEL	*Youth Aliya* worker, about 40.
ZABRODSKY	caretaker of the castle, about 57.
LENA	a young woman, 19 years old.

SCENE
An old castle in a Central European country.
The same setting is used throughout the play.

TIME
September 1947, some two years after the Second World War.

Act I takes place between 9 & 10 p.m;
Act II—between 10 & 11 p.m.;
Act III—between 11 p.m. and midnight.

ACT I

[*The library. Bookcases along the walls. Paintings by old masters and tapestries. One window with heavy curtains (which are now open). Two medium sized tables and deep-set arm-chairs. A sofa. On one of the tables—an electric kettle and tea service for two. On the second (by the sofa)—a telephone. A librarian's ladder by the right bookcase. Above the wall tapestry, between the bookcases, center, an old cuckoo clock. Doors to the right and left.*

A rainy, stormy evening with occasional lightning and thunder. Sand, Zabrodsky and Dora are standing in the room. Dora carries a raincoat on her arm and a briefcase in her hand.]

SAND: I'm very sorry, Mr. Zabrodsky, but we have no choice. We must impose on your hospitality tonight.

ZABRODSKY: [*Unrelenting*] I'm only the caretaker here. I have no authority to lodge strangers for the night.

SAND: But what shall we do?

ZABRODSKY: I would advise you to ring up the city; perhaps those who sent you will be kind enough to propose some solution...

DORA: At this hour!

SAND: I've already tried to call up. The line is cut. Probably because of the storm. I'd be very grateful if you...

ZABRODSKY: I have no authority.

SAND: [*Forcefully*]. The government's instructions, which I handed over to you, explicitly say that you are to place the library at my disposal and render all possible assistance. I think that also covers the possibility of lodging here in the case of an emergency. Look what's going on outside! And there's plenty of room here!

247

ZABRODSKY: This castle is now a museum. It is not customary to sleep in a museum. And… you have brought a guest, of whom no mention is made in the instructions…

DORA: [*A bit hurt; hesitantly*]. Really, Sand, maybe we should try to go!

SAND: You're out of your mind! Look! It's sixty kilometers to the nearest town. And you know what the condition of the car is… [*A thunderclap cuts him short*].

ZABRODSKY: [*Seeing he has no choice in the matter*]. I quite understand, sir, that it is difficult to travel now. But the castle, is a museum…. There are no sleeping accommodations…and when one is only an employee responsible to the authorities, a mere caretaker…one hesitates to violate the law…[*Thunder*].

SAND: But on such a night the law wouldn't force even a dog out of doors!

ZABRODSKY: Not so, my dear sir, nowadays the law dispatches men to perdition—without the slightest qualm.

SAND: And are you the representative of the law here?

ZABRODSKY: Hardly. I'm its victim.

SAND: Ah, it's not such a terrible offense. Nobody will jail you for not throwing people out on a stormy night. If you wish, I'll go over to the Ministry tomorrow, as soon as I get to town, and explain the whole matter to them… at any rate, we're not leaving this place tonight! Well?

ZABRODSKY: [*Cornered*]. Well, then, you have no need of my consent—but please do not think it is a question of ill will on my part—after all, there are no accommodations at all in the castle, no beds, no linens or anything of that sort… and I… rather thought that some hotel along the highway would be more to the lady's taste.

DORA: I would really prefer some country inn…

ZABRODSKY: For that very reason I suggested…

DORA: Old castles are quite beautiful but not to live in…

ZABRODSKY: [*Staring at her*]. I see! [*Listens to the thunder*]. Please sit down! [*Dora sits down, Sand stands*].

SAND: [*To* DORA]. Really, Dora, I'm terribly sorry… I only meant to show you the castle… And now I'm afraid it's all been a bother to you. And what's more—we're a burden on Mr. Zabrodsky…

ZABRODSKY: No, not at all. I will arrange everything for you immediately… Would you like to lie down and rest?

DORA: Now! At nine o'clock?!

ZABRODSKY: Yes, yes… it is still quite early. If you would prefer to sit here awhile, please do so. [*To* SAND].
Why are you standing, sir? Please sit down. You are my guests now. [SAND *sits down*].

DORA: Unexpected guests are a nuisance, I know.

ZABRODSKY: I shall see to the arrangements. When you wish to retire, please call me. I shall be in my room, below. [*To* SAND]. You know where that is, sir.

SAND: Thank you very much.—And forgive us for having forced ourselves on you, Mr. Zabrodsky, but we really had no choice.

ZABRODSKY: No matter, no matter… [*Turns to go, hesitates by the doorway*]. But, nonetheless, perhaps you are tired?

SAND: No, no! And if you're not tired, Mr. Zabrodsky, and if you don't mind spending an evening with strangers, why we'd be very happy if you'd stay on with us.

ZABRODSKY: That is very kind of you. [*Approaches them, but does not sit down*].

SAND: [*To Dora*]. That's how life knocks one about! Wars, storms, upheavals… and one is always a burden on somebody, unintentionally, against one's will. [*To* ZABRODSKY]. Won't you sit down, sir? [*Zabrodsky continues to stand*].

SAND: [*To Dora*]. By force of accident you break into a different world and then find yourself captive. [*Looks around the room*]. But what a wonderful captivity! I would be willing to stay on in this library for many months… with these books and these paintings.…

DORA: [*To* ZABRODSKY]. Please don't be frightened. Whenever he sees books, he can't tear himself away. But we won't impose on you more than absolutely necessary. I'll see to that. We'll leave tomorrow morning at dawn. I must get back to the city early.

ZABRODSKY: [*Courteously*]. Why no, on the contrary.... I hope you will enjoy your stay here.... Please do not blame me for my rudeness. It is many years since I have had the pleasure of entertaining guests. Living alone in a forest, one becomes uncivilized and uncourteous.

SAND: Why, not at all. We are the ones who should apologize, not you.... But won't you sit down, please?

ZABRODSKY: [*Standing*] And you are most probably hungry and thirsty—would you like some tea?

SAND: It's very kind of you, but...

ZABRODSKY: No, no, it is no trouble at all...

DORA: Tea, now, in this storm and cold... that would be wonderful. [*Bends over the kettle*]. Well, this is a woman's job... [*Raises the cover of the kettle*]. Yes, but water...

ZABRODSKY: I will bring some immediately...

DORA: Please, sir, if you'd like us to feel at home, then let me fetch the water. At the end of the corridor, behind the small room [*points at the door*], I noticed a tap...

ZABRODSKY: [*Trying to suppress his indignation*]. I see that Madame has already made a thorough survey of the castle...

DORA: [*Sensing his anger*]. While Mr. Sand was busy in the library, I looked over the rooms a bit. I didn't know it was forbidden...

ZABRODSKY: Why, not at all.

DORA: Tea, with your permission... [*Takes the kettle and starts for the door*].

ZABRODSKY: But nevertheless, Madame, perhaps I... [DORA *exits*].

SAND: [*After Dora leaves the room*]. Don't worry about her, sir, she'll find her way. Her work has taught her to get along in strange places. Do sit down, please! [*Short pause.* ZABRODSKY *sits.* SAND, *at a loss to open the conversation, surveys the books*]. What a wonderful collection!

ZABRODSKY: I am very pleased, sir, that you have found books that are of interest to you.... Have you had time to examine all of them?

SAND: No, there are still two shelves [*Rises*]—these two—ah, when I come to places like these and see such a library—such fine libraries in which the Nazis did as they pleased, vandalizing books which were collected here over generations...

ZABRODSKY: You are quite right, they did as they pleased...

SAND: [*Goes over to the shelf*]. Here is a first edition of Voltaire—and they ripped off the covers... what for?

ZABRODSKY: They turned the leather covers into pocket-books for their mistresses.

SAND: I can't look at such things calmly.... It makes my blood boil...

ZABRODSKY: I quite understand your feeling, after all, you are a librarian!

SAND: As a matter of fact, I'm *not* a librarian...

ZABRODSKY: But the official instructions describe you as...

SAND: Yes, I now have to deal with books again, [*Laughs*].
Oh, I didn't come here under false pretenses! [*Sees Zabrod-sky's anxiety*]. You see, sir, in our country you will hardly find anyone who has stuck to the same profession during all these years. I've changed mine quite often... I used to be a librarian—and then our country needed farmers, so I went to a collective settlement; the children grew up and had to be educated—so I became a teacher; then, back to the land again; when the war came—I turned soldier; when the war was over—back to farming.
[*Shows his hands*]. Here, look at my hands...

ZABRODSKY: [*Smiles*]. "The hands are the hands of Esau..."
[SAND *looks at him*]. Isn't that how the Bible puts it?

SAND: Yes, indeed.

ZABRODSKY: And now you have again turned librarian?

SAND: For a short while. I was slightly wounded during the war, and afterwards I went back home, to the fields...

ZABRODSKY: Perhaps I had best go and show the lady where the water is!

SAND: No. Why bother? She'll find it!

ZABRODSKY: Are you sure?

SAND: Of course, I told you she's accustomed to strange houses—that's part of her job.

ZABRODSKY: I see... ah, please excuse the interruption... you said you were wounded during the war and then went home.

SAND: Yes, and then the wound acted up again. I've been disqualified for physical labor and I don't have the patience to sit around in a convalescent home. Recently we learned that many of the books that were stolen from Jewish libraries in Germany, were scattered about by the Nazis in this country. I've been sent here to track them down and ship them to our National Library in Jerusalem... it's a wonderful vacation for me—without being a complete waste of time.

ZABRODSKY: And so you travel from castle to castle.

SAND: From library to library and from castle to castle, and the more remote the place, the greater the surprises. And that intrigues me. I'm a hunter by nature, you know, a book hunter.

ZABRODSKY: [*Looking at the door through which Dora left the room*]. And the lady?

SAND: She's searching out Jewish children who survived the war...

ZABRODSKY: Fascinating. And where does she look for them?

SAND: Everywhere—in the homes of peasants who sheltered them from the Nazis, in remote villages, in convents...

ZABRODSKY: Most interesting...and you, sir, help her in this search?

SAND: I? No, I just happened to meet her in the capital. We're childhood friends. Her work had exhausted her and I offered to entertain her by bringing her here to see this beautiful castle.

ZABRODSKY: [*Smiling*]. You make it sound as if only she works while you rest!

SAND: My work is much easier. The books follow me very willingly.

ZABRODSKY: Ah. Then the children do not follow her as willingly?

SAND: That's not what I said. But there are all kinds of cases, there are children who have become accustomed over the years to the way of life which the war forced on them...

ZABRODSKY: And they refuse to follow her—to your country?

SAND: There *are* such cases.... But ultimately I believe they all go with her. She has one invincible ally.

ZABRODSKY: Indeed? And who is that?

SAND: The healthy instincts of the children themselves, their feeling for life, their will to live, even after the war has destroyed half their lives...

ZABRODSKY: Most interesting... [*Looks at the door*].

SAND: I found her almost completely exhausted. A most unfortunate thing happened to her last week. Ah, it's terrible work! I myself worked with children like these during the war... [*Notices that Zabrodsky is not paying any attention to him*]... but I'm afraid you're tired of listening...

ZABRODSKY: [*Absently, his eyes glued to the door*]. Why, no, on the contrary, on the contrary... [*Enter* DORA].

DORA: Here's the water... please excuse me... I lost my way at first. I couldn't find the light.

ZABRODSKY: [*Rises*]. Yes, yes, it is entirely my fault, Madame. I should have gone instead. I know my way about this house even in the dark.

DORA: [*Plugging in the kettle*]. But the table is only set for two... [*Sits down*].

ZABRODSKY: And you are two, Madame. [*Sits down*].

SAND: No, no, Mr. Zabrodsky, we won't have tea without you...

ZABRODSKY: As a matter of fact, I...

SAND: Really, it's out of the question. I beg of you.

ZABRODSKY: If you insist.... It is a long time since I have had the pleasure of entertaining guests. A solitary old man, practically a recluse, in this manor which is buried in a virgin forest so to speak... yes... the table is always set for two here... that is, when they notify me that one person is coming. Madame's arrival [*With exaggerated courtesy*] was a pleasant surprise. With your permission, I shall fetch another cup.

SAND: We're sorry to trouble you. [ZABRODSKY *goes to the right door, bows and is about to exit. Thunder*].

ZABRODSKY: [*Murmurs to the thunder, with his face to the window*]. "And the stars of heaven fell unto earth, even as a fig tree casteth her untimely figs, when she is shaken of a mighty wind." [*Exits*].

DORA: What did he say?

SAND: Nothing... a verse from the New Testament.

DORA: Awful! Till I found the light in this labyrinth… Oh, damn it, Sand, all this unnerves me… I want to go home…

SAND: You know that's impossible now, Dora. I'm sorry. Dora, you must stop thinking about it. It's not your fault that the boy committed suicide. [*Begins climbing the ladder*].

DORA: Yes, yes…it wasn't my fault, wasn't my fault… I know… but…where are you climbing to?

SAND: Excuse me a moment, Dora. I haven't gone over these books yet, up here… [*Climbs up*].

DORA: You and your books! In such a storm… and you don't give a hang! I can't stand it! And this old man, with his verses from the New Testament.

SAND: [*On top of the ladder. Pulls out a book and mumbles to himself*]. Interesting. These books hardly have any dust on them. Somebody's been reading them.

DORA: Leave the books alone for a moment! I tell you that here… maybe we can still get out of here!

SAND: [*On the ladder*]. If I could do anything for you…

DORA: Really, I don't know what's come over me. This old man! I'm afraid of him. It's as if he—rose up from the grave!

SAND: No, it's nothing at all. All caretakers of castles and museums are queer birds… I rather like him, seems to be well educated. Who knows what he used to be.

DORA: Yes, who knows! And did you notice how he tried to get us out of here! And there are no accommodations at all here [*imitating him*] "no linens or anything of that sort!" And now, all of a sudden he has everything! An electric kettle, and hot water and cups, everything!

SAND: [*Leafing through a book*]. What's the trouble, Dora?

DORA: And what high-flown talk! "I haven't had the pleasure of entertaining guests"—as if the castle were his! If only we could get out of here!

SAND: I'm rather pleased that the storm has held us up here. Two more shelves to go—I'll work a bit tonight, and that'll save me an extra trip.

DORA: But what will I do here?

SAND: You go to sleep and rest. It'll do you good.

DORA: Sleep! In this place! [*Thunder*]. You don't understand anything!

SAND: [*Goes down to her. Worried*]. What's come over you, Dora? What's happened to you all of a sudden?

DORA: [*Laughs nervously*]. I don't know. I want to go home.

SAND: But how can we get home now?

DORA: I told you you don't understand. I don't mean the hotel in town. I want to go home, really home. To *my* house! To the heat and the khamsin! This castle is only one stop along the way... I was born here, I grew up here, I spent my childhood here. And suddenly—it's all so unreal, so strange and alien! The cities, the villages, the monasteries—they're no longer real to me! My home is in Palestine!

SAND: So is mine, Dora. There are such moments of nostalgia on every trip, I know. [*Turns back to the books*].

DORA: No you don't! Because this country is really strange for you! But for me—this was once home! And then these children—day in, day out, I have to talk them into leaving this country... while I stay on here—in this world.... I want to go home so badly!

SAND: [*On the ladder*]. And do you think that I don't want to go back!

DORA: But you'll go back!

SAND: So will you.

DORA: Yes, yes, But with you it's different! [*Calms down a bit*]. With you everything is always under control. You always know your way, you always find your place. You'll leave at the right time and go back at the right time. [*Flaring up again*]. And you'll always be calm and wise and sure of yourself... I used to think myself a practical person, I used to think I would always face up to reality! But this weariness! This storm! This old man! No, I can't bear it! I've known you for twenty years already and I've never yet seen you lose your head! It can drive one mad! I don't understand how your wife stands it!

SAND: [*Laughs*]. Well, as a matter of fact, it does upset her. It upsets all the women…

ZABRODSKY: [*Enters with cup, plates and biscuits*]. We are in for a fine night! [DORA *rises and goes toward him to help him*].

ZABRODSKY: [*Sees* SAND *at the top of the ladder*]. I see, sir, that you are still searching for hidden treasures up there!

DORA: [*To* SAND]. Really, Sand, it's time you came down! Let's have some tea!

SAND: [*Descending*]. Yes, yes… [*Takes plates from* ZABRODSKY *and carries them to the table.* SAND *sits down.* DORA *begins to set the table*].

ZABRODSKY: With your permission, Madame. [*Sits down*]. I'm afraid there is a difficulty that I cannot overcome. The adjoining room, here [*points at the left door*] is completely furnished… that will be for you, Madame. But the rest of the rooms are kept as a museum. However, I would be glad to place my room at your disposal, sir. I hope you will be comfortable.

SAND: No, thank you very much. I'll stay here, in the library. There's a sofa here and I don't need any bedding.

ZABRODSKY: That is out of the question. This is no place to sleep, and I am really accustomed to anything and everything.

SAND: So am I, Mr. Zabrodsky: In my travels during the war, and before that as well, I slept on benches, crates, tables, floors…

ZABRODSKY: All the more reason you should sleep in a bed tonight; we're at peace now, you know. People say the war is over.

SAND: No, Mr. Zabrodsky, I'll remain here…

ZABRODSKY: My room is narrow and most modest, but nonetheless, it is a bedroom…

SAND: No, we've been enough of a bother as it is!

ZABRODSKY: Bother! Why you have worked all day long!

SAND: And that's precisely why I'll be happy to spend my night here. I haven't finished my work and there are still two shelves over there to be examined.

ZABRODSKY: [*The issue is obviously important to him*]. I do not think you will find anything of interest there: only the family archives which the owner of the castle left behind.

SAND: I'm familiar with this sort of thing! Just where you don't expect to find anything, you discover the most amazing treasures. No, don't insist...

ZABRODSKY: But...

DORA: The water is boiling! [*Begins to pour tea into Zabrodsky's cup*].

ZABRODSKY: Thank you very much, Madame! [*To* SAND]. But you really should not work all night!

SAND: I'll work a bit and then I'll lie down to rest! [*To* DORA, *who has served his tea*]. Thank you!

ZABRODSKY: How can you possibly rest here in this storm—and where will you lie down?

DORA: [*Pours out her tea; to herself*]. Now for a cup of hot tea—it's wonderful! I can't get used to the weather here, and they say this is a hot summer!

ZABRODSKY: This sofa is short! [*To* DORA, *who serves him biscuits*]. Thank you very much. [*To* SAND]. Much too short!

DORA: [*Offering biscuits to Sand*]. Please have some... [*To* ZABRODSKY]. Back home, September is one continuous heat wave. It's unbearably hot even at night!

ZABRODSKY: Really?

DORA: When I think that I once loved the frost... [*Drinks her tea*].

ZABRODSKY: Well then, sir?

DORA: And now my teeth chatter at the very thought of it... brrr!

SAND: [*To* ZABRODSKY]. It's very kind of you, Mr. Zabrodsky: But, really, I'm doing this for myself, not for you. I've become attached to this library room—here, in the shadow of these wonderful books—all these riches—I would be quite willing to sleep even on the floor! [DORA *surveys the room again as Sand speaks; it is obvious that she does not share his opinion.* ZABRODSKY *sighs*].

DORA: [*Sipping her tea*]. But you're not drinking! [*They begin to drink*]. Incidentally, we never used to drink tea. We always drank coffee. Only "fashionable society" drank tea... [*Listens to the wind*]. And this is how you live here, Mr. Zabrodsky?

ZABRODSKY: This is how I live.

DORA: And you're not afraid?

ZABRODSKY: What should I be afraid of?

DORA: It's far from town, and the loneliness, and all these old things…

ZABRODSKY: Old things!

DORA: Yes, yes, I know, fashionable people like to think that the older the object, the more beautiful it is.

SAND: But they really are beautiful!

DORA: [*Looking around*]. These enormous rooms… it's beautiful, but not to live in!

ZABRODSKY: Yes, Madame, you have already said that, if I am not mistaken.

DORA: Really?

ZABRODSKY: But people lived here, spent all their lives here, and lived well! And their lives were immeasurably more beautiful and full than the lives of those who inhabit these modern boxes…

SAND: As for beauty—I quite agree. But as for fullness—we should ask the people themselves, those who used to live here; or rather, we should have asked them then, not now. After all, what do we know about them!

DORA: And as for those modern boxes—they, at least, have the virtue of not collecting centuries of dust, and a great many people can live in them.

ZABRODSKY: Certainly, everything is polished there, smooth and electrical! Above all—electrical!

DORA: Well, right here, you now seem to have an electric kettle as well as a telephone.

ZABRODSKY: But there is also something else here.

DORA: For instance?

ZABRODSKY: [*Explaining to her as if to a child*]. You see, Madame, I can introduce an electric kettle and a telephone into this ancient castle—it will bear it. But try to introduce this tapestry or this old bookcase into one of your modern, low-roofed crates—it simply can't be done! It would be ludicrous! Your crate would fall to pieces!… These modern lives, all cast in one mould, cannot tolerate beauty.

SAND: Yes, perhaps we no longer have any feeling for that sort of thing. Perhaps we've forgotten something in our haste. These old books—look how beautiful they are! Even the typeface...

DORA: I've heard this tune before. Everything was better in the good old days! And these lovely books of yours, these wonderful manuscripts—who saw them? How many people read them?

ZABRODSKY: [*Ironically*]. Yes, now very many people read books!

DORA: You mean that the covers are dirty and sticky and the pages are soiled, and the writing is cheap! Of course!

ZABRODSKY: And all of them standardized products, the literature as well as the houses!

DORA: Yes, it's all very nice to visit the Old City of Jerusalem or the Ghetto of Prague and then to rave about the beauty of the antiquities! But let these same aesthetes try to live in those picturesque ruins! Let them try it for one week—why people live their entire lives there! I've seen it with my own eyes! I've been to those places!

SAND: But we weren't speaking of ruins, Dora! We were speaking of a castle.

DORA: [*In full swing, not to be restrained*]. Castles and ruins are always found side by side! Perhaps I have no aesthetic sense. Perhaps I've witnessed too much sorrow and anguish and poverty during these years, tracking down these poor children, homeless, delinquent, infected with vermin and T.B., but I hate all this old stuff, all this useless ash!

SAND: What's that got to do with it?

DORA: I love sunshine and cleanliness, and I want people to be able to live a healthy, simple life! Yes! People! As for all the rest, I don't care if...

SAND: Dora!

DORA: [*Suddenly notices that Zabrodsky is listening*]. Here... I mean, there are really beautiful things here. I beg your pardon. I must be overtired.... I've exaggerated, of course.... I once loved these things, too. Perhaps I still love them.

SAND: [*To* ZABRODSKY]. As far as I'm concerned, this is one of the most beautiful castles I've seen, and I've been through quite a number lately.... I can't take my eyes off that clock. It's French, I believe?

ZABRODSKY: I see you are quite a connoisseur.

SAND: Hardly.

ZABRODSKY: Very few identify it correctly by sight: there are similar clocks in Saxony.

SAND: [*Laughs*]. I have a weakness for old clocks. My father was a watchmaker, and cuckoo-clocks are a childhood love. Does it work?

ZABRODSKY: No, it's out of order. [*Changing the subject*]. Tomorrow morning I will gladly show you a very fine Saxonian clock. It is kept in that chest, there, below... When you get up tomorrow morning...

DORA: No, no! Please, Mr. Zabrodsky, don't show him anything tomorrow. If he starts looking at clocks and books we'll never get out of here. And I think you've had quite enough, with us spending the entire night here.

ZABRODSKY: I hope you will have a pleasant sleep here tonight, Madame.

DORA: I'm not so sure. The castle isn't haunted, is it?

ZABRODSKY: [*Seriously*]. Of course. All old castles are haunted!

DORA: Then I'll really have a pleasant sleep! I'll dream about all the English novels I read as a child. Sand, I'm sure you never read ghost stories!

SAND: No, I read travel books and Indian stories!

DORA: Then you haven't the faintest idea!

SAND: I can very well imagine: "And at night, when the clock in the tower struck twelve times, and all the inhabitants of the castle were deep in sleep, there appeared the ghost of the beauteous Lady of the Castle"... is that it?

DORA: Exactly! When I was thirteen, those ghosts wouldn't let me shut my eyes at night!

ZABRODSKY: There is nothing fearful about ghosts. [ZABRODSKY *rises, goes over to the window, lowers the heavy curtain. Mumbles to himself*]. "And there followed hail and fire mingled with blood, and they we cast upon the earth."

DORA: [*To* SAND]. I'll always remember the chill that used to grip me when I read those novels. Ghosts walking through the night; and secret doors opening, and choked voices howling from the cellar…

SAND: Naturally! If the castle is haunted by ghosts, it stands to reason that there should be hidden cellars and labyrinths and secret doors in the walls. I'm sure you'll find all these here as well.

ZABRODSKY: [*Still standing by the window, his back turned*]. No, there are no hidden cellars and secret doors here. [*Turns and goes back to his place*].

SAND: Don't be so sure. Why in Wallenstein Manor, just a few months ago, they discovered two secret trap doors under the matting in the mistress's room.

DORA: [*Laughing*] Two!

SAND: She probably had to hide her lover from her husband, as well as one lover from another! That's what I call living! [*To Zabrodsky*]. So you see, Mr. Zabrodsky, never say "no" until you've checked and rechecked.

ZABRODSKY: I am thoroughly familiar with this house.

SAND: You never know, you never know! How long have you been serving as caretaker of this castle?

ZABRODSKY: [*Ironically*]. I have been serving as caretaker of this castle ever since private property was nationalized in this country.

SAND: Well, that's not so long: a year or a year and a half at most. You can't get to know a castle like this in such a short time.

ZABRODSKY: Quite correct, sir.

SAND: [*Joking*]. Well, then, perhaps we'll all spend the night together examining all the entrances, all the wings—who knows… [*Rises.* ZABRODSKY *makes an imperative gesture, which forces him down again*].

ZABRODSKY: I have no need to examine this castle. I know it—and I knew it before I became its caretaker. I knew it from the day I came into this world. I knew it from my mother's womb. I know every corner in it, every crack. This castle, sir, belonged to me. To my father's fathers and to their ancestors. This was my home. [*Silence.* ZABRODSKY *rises. Collects the dishes and places them on the tray*].

ZABRODSKY: [*Quietly and dryly*]. With your permission, I will prepare the bed for the lady. [*Exits*].

SAND: [*As* ZABRODSKY *leaves*]. Mr. Zabrod... [*But* ZABRODSKY *has closed the door behind him. A prolonged silence between Sand and Dora*].

DORA: Really embarrassing... who could have guessed...

SAND: Terrible!

DORA: From the very beginning I didn't want to stay here...

SAND: Nonsense! That has nothing to do with it!

DORA: I told you we should try to leave...

SAND: There you go again!

DORA: If we had left, all this wouldn't have happened...

SAND: I'll go find him...

DORA: You will not.... I don't want to stay here alone! And after all, what did we really do?

SAND: Don't you see what we did?

DORA: What if he is the owner of the castle, can't I say what I think!

SAND: Ah, what *you* said doesn't matter!

DORA: Then what are you so excited about? It's slightly embarrassing. I agree, but why get all worked up?

SAND: Ah, Dora, don't you understand? First I ask him: "How long have you been serving here as caretaker"—and then I begin explaining to him, you understand—I explain to *him*, that in such a short time it's impossible to know the castle!

DORA: But you couldn't have known who he was!

SAND: I should have sensed how much he loves this place—and all these things. I don't care at all if he's the owner of the castle... that's not the question! You just don't talk this way to a man about the things that are dearest to him.

DORA: My God, Sand, what do you know about the things that are dear to him? What do you know about him at all?

SAND: What I know is enough for me...

DORA: But not for me. First of all, I want to know what this man did during the war, when the Nazis were here...

SAND: [*With assurance*]. This man, no! Not him!

DORA: Don't be naïve, Sand; I've seen lots of people these past months.

SAND: So have I. And I tell you—not this man!

DORA: And I tell you: Look at this library, that you've been fussing about all day long—were the Nazis here or not?

SAND: They were…

DORA: And where was he?

ZABRODSKY: [*Enters as she completes her question. He is completely calm*]. I have placed the linens in Madame's room. The adjoining room is the washroom. The towels are there. [DORA *and* SAND *rise as he enters. He advances to the center of the stage, as if to turn out the lights. To* SAND]. Shall I light the upper shelves for you, sir?

DORA: Mr. Zabrodsky, please forgive me…

SAND: Do forgive us, that idiotic joke about secret doors…

DORA: Why everything we said—we didn't mean to—it wasn't meant personally…

ZABRODSKY: Please do not apologize, Madame, how could it possibly have been personal?

SAND: But if we have offended you—you must understand that we had no such intention, we couldn't possibly…

ZABRODSKY: Far from it, sir, I am no longer vulnerable to offense… Why do you not sit down? Won't you sit down, please… and if I am in the way….

DORA: No, no, of course not…

ZABRODSKY: Please sit down, Madame… [DORA *goes over hesitantly to her place.* SAND *continues to stand*].

SAND: I fell into a manner of speech…

ZABRODSKY: [*Looks at him, begins to smile*]. You amaze me, sir! Why, that is the accepted manner of speech nowadays. No one has spoken to me otherwise—for many years…

SAND: But I beg your forgiveness… I didn't want to talk that way!

ZABRODSKY: Yes, yes… I am quite aware of that. Generally, when people come here—they talk and I do not listen. I stopped listening to what people say—long ago, long ago! And if I deviated from my custom tonight, sir, it was only because, at first, you spoke a different language. I began to listen... that is the essential... and as for the rest—let it be forgotten, do sit down, please!

SAND: [*Hesitates*]. Only if I am certain that you've forgiven me!

ZABRODSKY: But what is it that troubles you! Nothing has come between us. [*In order to prove that, he sits down.* SAND *follows suit. Once again—a moment of uneasy silence*].

DORA: And what I said about this house...

ZABRODSKY: [*Brushing it away*]. Ah, could it be otherwise? Who still understands nowadays—what it means to stay, to live [*With a wide gesture, encompassing the castle*] in such a house!

SAND: Yes, we've led a different kind of life, Mr. Zabrodsky, our past is different... [ZABRODSKY *is silent*]. But one thing I can imagine to myself: What it means to live always with these books. Was the library always here?

ZABRODSKY: Yes, always.

DORA: [*Also looking at the library*]. It must be very old?

ZABRODSKY: Very.

SAND: Today, while I worked here, I kept thinking to myself: With what devotion these books were collected here! Even after the vandalism of the Germans, you still feel how generation after generation played its part here... such a sure instinct, such fine taste...

ZABRODSKY: Yes, that is true.

SAND: And there are more precious old books here than in any library I've seen.

ZABRODSKY: The uncle of my father's grandfather—the Bishop—was a distinguished scholar; most of the old books are his.

SAND: Ah, is that his portrait below, in the drawing room?

ZABRODSKY: No, that is Cardinal Morelli. My mother's cousin. His father was Italian.

SAND: Cardinal Morelli? The one who wrote the new commentary on St. John's Revelation? That was published in Rome—in 1882, if I'm not mistaken? I believe he also had some connection with the royal house?

ZABRODSKY: Ah, you are most learned, sir! Yes, he was Her Majesty's father's confessor. *Him* I still remember. [*Smiling to a distant memory*]. When I was eight years old he presented me to the Empress…she was a charming woman, the Empress—and she did not fancy me at all. "This child"—she said—"this child has stubborn eyes." Yes, that is what she said… that was Cardinal Morelli. And this is the Bishop. [*Rises, picks up a miniature and shows it to* SAND]. He lived in the eighteenth century.

SAND: [*Looks from the miniature to* ZABRODSKY]. He resembles you.

ZABRODSKY: Yes, so they say. The Bishop was an ardent Voltairian, extremely free-minded, a philosopher and naturalist…

DORA: [*Who has not looked at the picture*]. That's something that has always puzzled me—how could these priests and monks possibly reconcile religion with science!

SAND: [*Fearing that Dora will give the conversation a wrong twist*]. And the old books, then, are his?

ZABRODSKY: Yes, this entire section of the library. Fortunately, the Nazis did not touch it…

SAND: Ah those books—the first editions—

ZABRODSKY: Yes, he collected them—

SAND: The parchment bindings—and the faded letters—

ZABRODSKY: The faded letters—

DORA: [*Caught up in the mood of the conversation*]. The faded letters! We had such books in our house. My father said they were inherited from the Maharal of Prague.… I never read them. Neither did my father. But my grandfather.… I was very small.… I remember grandfather's white beard… he was always poring over some book… I don't know what he was reading. I used to be afraid to go up to him—not always, only when he was reading…it seemed as if there was such a silence in the house when he bent over these books… once, I remember it so clearly, a mouse came out and started to roam around the room—and I was terribly frightened. But I was afraid to scream out, because grandfather was reading and it was so quiet… I didn't know how to read, but I still remember the faded letters and the heavy bindings…

ZABRODSKY: Yes, faded letters and heavy bindings… so! This grand-
father of yours, Madame, whom you described so well, knew
the significance of such books. If he were to come here, he
would perhaps understand—more than all the professors of
history and art…. Did you also have such a grandfather, sir?

SAND: My grandfather was a poor Jew. A watchmaker, like my father.
But he also had books, which he inherited from his father.

ZABRODSKY: Yes, I once knew such old Jews… [*Pauses, surveys the
books and the room*]. Not fit to live in! Why, look here, sir, one
may also come to you, to the Holy Land, to your city of Jeru-
salem, and say: "All this is very nice, but not fit to live in! This
is history, archaeology, antiquity… but not fit to live in! But
you Jews, don't you claim that no country is as fit for living
in as yours? Precisely because it is part of an old tradition. Yes,
perhaps that is why I broke my silence tonight and spoke to
you. I think the Jews are the only ones in the world today who
are still capable of understanding the meaning of tradition.

SAND: This is the second time tonight, sir, that you astound me with
your knowledge of my people.

ZABRODSKY: I know very little. But I have always admired the Jewish
people for not succumbing to the vanities and fashions of this
world, for persisting on its own way. I saw this people in its
agony during these years.

DORA: You were not the only one who saw, sir. The whole world saw.
They saw and kept quiet and didn't raise a finger!

ZABRODSKY: The world? But what could you expect from such a
world? Deaf and dumb and dull-hearted. And the dead walk-
ing amongst the living. And I was at first among the dead. It
is written in St. John's Revelation: "The last, which was dead,
and is alive"—I am that man.

DORA: [*Looks at Sand with a questioning silence*].

ZABRODSKY: This is not mysticism. These are hard facts, to which we
can all attest. I ask you: What is the sign of life? That a man
eats and drinks and moves? Not at all! How many dead walk
amongst us on the earth—sleep at night and rise in the morn-
ing—without knowing that they are dead. I, at least, knew.

To live, you see, is to take part in the deeds of this world, whether one is moved by love or hate or heart's desire—but if this is lacking, then it is death. Is this not the truth?

SAND: Yes, it is.

ZABRODSKY: Well, then. In 1918 the life I loved came to an end. The Empire was gone and what are we with all our titles and castles, without the Empire which was the crown of our existence from the very first? Nothing but ghosts, yes, ghosts! [*Looks piercingly at Dora, who shrinks under his gaze as if chilled to the marrow*]. Of course, there were also those who, without much ado, instantly found the way to that other world—the one in which we now have the good fortune to live. I remember, one fine day, a friend of mine and of my father's came to me and said: "What a pity you didn't manage to sell that tapestry a month ago to America. Now the price has gone down considerably!" This tapestry, to America! I thought he had lost his wits—but as it turned out, he and his like thought me the witless one! Why, after the war, I came back to my castle, penniless. Conclusive proof that I should have sold all these things—to America! Or better yet—to the war profiteers who had grown rich!! And I—yes, what did I have left to do in such a world? It no longer had any meaning. And without meaning—there can be no life. So I died. It was an easy death, comparatively speaking. In this part of the world, they did not yet molest people like myself; we were respected, even venerated.... Yes, and I continued to eat, drink, sleep, move, but as a matter of fact I was dead—buried in this castle like an Egyptian King embalmed in his pyramid... but even death is not eternal in this world! [*Sinks into silence*].

SAND: [*To break the silence*]. Because, in the final reckoning, people who eat and drink, especially those who have not forfeited their spiritual world—are alive.

ZABRODSKY: Sometimes! [*To* DORA]. You asked me before, Madame, whether ghosts haunt this castle. Well, now you see such a one before your very eyes. But I am no longer dangerous. I am not dangerous!

267

DORA: [*Somehow uneasy*]. I don't know… I'm not sure.

ZABRODSKY: That I am alive?

DORA: No… not that…

ZABRODSKY: [DORA *keeps quiet*]. That I'm not dangerous?

DORA: [*Gathering courage*]. Yes!

ZABRODSKY: But how can a weak, old man possibly endanger anyone?

DORA: [*At first still somewhat confused, but she pulls herself together and says angrily*]. I don't know. I'm not at all sure of it. But I wanted to ask… [*cuts herself short*].

ZABRODSKY: You wanted to ask a question, Madame?

DORA: And where were you all these years? During the war?

ZABRODSKY: [*Quietly and dryly*]. Here.

DORA: In your pyramid?

ZABRODSKY: If you wish… I was here. In the castle.

SAND: But… but—why—[*points at the books*]. The Nazis were here.

ZABRODSKY: Yes, they were here.

SAND: But—how is that? If you were here?

ZABRODSKY: I asked them over. The Nazi Headquarters was located here throughout the last year of the war. Until the liberation.

DORA: [*Gets up emphatically*].

ZABRODSKY: [*Ironically*]. Why, you understood at once, Madame, that I am one of them. Isn't that so?

DORA: [*His intonation puts her on her guard*]. Nowadays—everybody is suspect.

ZABRODSKY: Quite.

SAND: [*Sensing that there is something more to this, but still groping in the dark*]. But you just now said, sir—that you sat here with the Nazis during the war!

ZABRODSKY: I sat with them. I ate with them at one table, I heard their obscenities, I saw them carving their names in my furniture… [*As he speaks, his anger flares up…* DORA *does not yet grasp its meaning—but the light begins to dawn on* SAND].

DORA: And after all this you…

ZABRODSKY: And after all this…

SAND: Ah, Dora. Stop this, really! [*To* ZABRODSKY]. The German Headquarters? In this castle! The Headquarters, you said! But sir—then you must be... What a fool I am! You must excuse me, how could I possibly have missed the connection!... your name and the name of the castle...

ZABRODSKY: Ah, my good sir, that is all past. It is not worth recalling!

SAND: Then...then you're the man? You're the one they called the Count? But how could I have missed the connection?
[DORA *sits, looking with surprise form one to the other*].

ZABRODSKY: How could you possibly have guessed? I am surprised you know the story at all.

SAND: But it's a famous story. I heard it in Holland, when I was in Jewish Brigade... So you're the Count? And it was from here that you contacted the Underground?

ZABRODSKY: Yes. It was quite simple. Hate brought me to life. When the war broke out, I thought I could continue living apart from all those matters, I thought it had nothing to do with me...

DORA: Many thought so at first.

ZABRODSKY: Yes. I closed myself up here, to withdraw from the world, to live out the rest of my days in peace, far from all of them, from everything. But when I saw them here in the land of my fathers, when I set eyes on those officers, close-cropped, vulgar, ignorant, arrogant, prophesying the new life, setting up a new religion—a new religion of cannibals, a new life of savages, a new culture of swineherds! Always, it is always the scum of humanity, those who cannot grasp the ancient tradition and the true culture, who prophesy a new life, build another culture, and meanwhile they riot, murder, rape and spit on the carpets...

SAND: Yes, I understand. But how did it actually happen?

ZABRODSKY: The castle was abandoned, hidden in the forest. An ideal site for the General Headquarters. They took me into their confidence, and I passed on their secrets to the Underground which operated from the forest, not far from here.

The idiots! Just because I looked on complacently while they drank the wines from my father's cellar, pillaged my library, and wallowed in their vomit on these carpets... I detained them here until the very last moment. I handed them over, all of them, one by one, arms, plans and all...

SAND: Sir, it's a wonderful thing you did. Really, a most heroic act.

ZABRODSKY: [*Bitterly*]. And in recognition of this act they granted me a boon after the victory: they did not evict me like a stray dog to die in an alley. They did me a favour: They let me guard this castle—this "museum"—as they call it. To guard it—for them!

DORA: [*His bitterness has offended her*]. What can you expect, Mr. Zabrodsky, the regime changed after the war.

ZABRODSKY: [*More bitterly*]. Changed, Madame. Changed, very much so! For this we fought! We saved man's culture so that it could be turned—not into ruins, as the others had planned—but, according to the new dispensation—into lavatories!

DORA: Why are you so bitter? After all, you live in your castle, in your pyramid; what do you care if officially you're the owner or only the caretaker? Of course, maybe you can no longer have soirées here! But—let's say children were to come here, organized excursions from schools, and they would also have the chance of enjoying the beautiful things that were collected here for generations...

ZABRODSKY: Yes, the schools come. And quite often at that. And the teacher stands and shows them the "beautiful things," as you were kind enough to say, Madame, and delivers a talk about the cruelty and *ignorance* of those "feudal lords," who once lived here, until *they* came and rescued the people from oppression. *Feudal lords!* I, Madame, as you see, am a specimen of this genus; I am nothing but a remnant of the middle ages, the "dark" ages, that is to say... and the whole of life, the culture we painstakingly built generation after generation—why that was—so the young people are told—that was nothing but licentiousness, exploitation of down-trodden peasants, *jus primae noctis*... yes, that is how it was, Madame! No?

DORA: Yes. It was that, too…

SAND: Dora!

DORA: And those who lived here, who built this wonderful "culture," did they have any inkling of what was going on beyond the walls of their estates? Built a culture! And didn't take the trouble to move this culture one meter out of their castles! And now they turn up their noses because the visitors are not as refined as they are!

SAND: It's not a question of refinement, Dora!

DORA: As if I didn't know that! It's a question of everything, everything, everything that went on outside this castle for hundreds of years! At first people couldn't set foot here! They used dogs to guard places like these, to keep out intruders! And now that they're finally permitted to come in here—not only the children, but their teachers, and you and I—they're suddenly expected to behave as if they had lived *here,* and not in their tenements, all their lives! As if they were brought up by French governesses! And it's very good that they've finally come here! Very good! Now they'll begin to understand what was done to them and how they were forced to live, they'll begin to understand that now! And the "culture" will come in due time. I don't care if it takes even a hundred years. I've got plenty of time to wait, as long as people now have something to eat! Yes! And if you stay here, sir, as caretaker or owner—you're still living far better than all the others! And if the things they say are spoken to your face—as they are today or behind your back, as they were before—it doesn't make any difference at all! I don't see how it changes the facts!

ZABRODSKY: [*Dryly*]. There are many things you don't see, Madame. [*Rises*]. But I believe I must go. [*Thunder. All listen*]. You should rest now. What time is it? [SAND *looks at his watch,* DORA *at the wall clock*].

[*Together*]

SAND: Twenty to ten.

DORA: Ten.

ZABRODSKY: Ten o'clock?!

SAND: No. My watch is accurate. It's twenty of ten.

DORA: Ah, I looked at that wall clock which is out of order.

ZABRODSKY: So. [*Slight pause*]. I will make your bed, Madame, in the adjacent room. Here. [*Sighs*].

DORA: Thank you. If the linens are there, I'll make it myself.

ZABRODSKY: As you wish. [*Gathers up the tea dishes, places them on the tray. To* SAND]. Nevertheless, I do insist that you go down to my room.

SAND: No, really. Thank you very much.

ZABRODSKY: But you will be far more comfortable there. The storm is less audible there…

SAND: I like the sound of thunder, I'm an old storm-lover…

ZABRODSKY: But…

SAND: No, no… I won't take your bed! Under any circumstances!

ZABRODSKY: [*Shrugs his shoulders*]. Then I will at least remove the ladder to make the room look more livable.

SAND: No, please don't bother. I still want to look over the two shelves up there, to the right.

ZABRODSKY: Perhaps it would be wisest to put that off to the morning.

DORA: Tomorrow we leave at sunrise!

ZABRODSKY: [*Ignores her outburst. Controls himself. Dryly and politely*]. Well, then. The linens are already in Madame's room. [*Bows*]. Have a good rest—as good as possible in such a storm.

SAND: Good night. [ZABRODSKY *exits. Short Pause*].

DORA: Are you angry?

SAND: [*Silent*].

DORA: Why don't you answer me? Why are you keeping quiet? Oh, really! Didn't I feel it—you were embarrassed for me! I'm very sorry! You brought a guest with you and she doesn't know how to behave properly in the presence of princes and counts.

SAND: [*Sighs*].

DORA: As a matter of fact, why do you care at all? Tomorrow morning we'll leave the place and never see him again. Finished and done with.

SAND: Yes. Finished. We'll go—leaving behind an old, solitary man, who will remember to his dying day, that one night he broke his silence—perhaps for the first time in many years—to speak humanely to people, and they insulted him!

DORA: Humanely! And all this talk of "lavatories" sounds terribly "humane" to you!

SAND: I'm not obliged to prove myself personally in the right to everybody.

DORA: What do you mean personally in the right? And when he says—"It's always the scum of the earth that prophesies a new life!"

SAND: Why, he was talking about the Nazis!

DORA: Not only the Nazis, you know that very well.

SAND: Yes.

DORA: And to answer that—that, in your opinion, is insisting on being personally right!

SAND: Yes. Because the whole argument is superfluous. No good can come of it to anyone. His is a voice from the past. His past. He lives in it. He loves it. Then leave him be. We're already of a different time and different place. That's all.

DORA: And that's why you say *kaddish* and mourn at the grave of this splendid past, praying to God that He resurrect it! Well?

SAND: Only the son says *kaddish*. I'm no count's son. I, as you know, am the son of a Jewish watchmaker.

DORA: Such wit!

SAND: I'm not joking. I'm speaking quite seriously. I'm the son of a watchmaker and I'm personally interested, very much so, that the future be in the hands of the watchmakers and their children.

DORA: But you're completely captivated by this past.

SAND: The past, my dear, has many things which watchmakers' sons should also know, and even love. Even Zabrodsky's past. What to take from this past—that we'll decide for ourselves. But to argue with him about it? I don't want to. Why should I? *He* has the right to love what he loves and to hate what he hates. Don't you understand, Dora, that he's now obliged to speak the loftiest and bitterest words? This is his end. His tombstone. And we… there are very many of us—that's why we can afford to be mediocre and fulfill our obligations silently.

DORA: Ah, I don't understand all this philosophy! I'm scared, simply scared of being sentimental about this whole vanishing world. I was closer to it than you. And I know that its dangers aren't yet past.

SAND: Dangers!

DORA: Yes! If you had to deal with children hiding in strange families, in monasteries—you'd see how this "beauty" still grips them! Can you imagine what I go through every day? A constant war. The dead, with skeleton hands, have fastened on to living children, and are pulling them down to the grave.

SAND: But the living don't want to go down to the grave!

DORA: Ah! It's easy for you to talk! With your dead books! You pack them up and they follow you. But the children… I would gladly send you to do the terrible work I'm doing, then maybe you'd talk differently!

SAND: Dora, what *are* we quarreling about?

DORA: You're right. I'm tired. I'll go to sleep. Good night. [*Turns to the door*].

SAND: Good night, Dora.

DORA: [*Standing by the left door*]. And if Hamlet's father comes tonight, or Zabrodsky's great, great grandfather, General Zabrodsky—just call for help. I'm here in the next room.

SAND: [*Laughs*]. Ah, I'll manage on my own. Go to sleep, Dora, and have a good rest.

DORA: Yes, I need a rest. Good night. [*Exits*].

SAND: [*Puts out the center chandelier, so that the side lamp lights up only the right bookcase, against which the ladder is leaning, and throws a weak light on the center stage and the cuckoo clock. Sand whistles a quiet tune to himself and begins to mount the ladder to the books. But he changes his mind, goes down, and moves the ladder to the center, below the clock*]. Now let's have a look at this old clock! [*Climbs the ladder, opens the clock and pulls out a key*]. Ah, the key!

[*He winds the clock, which begins to play. Then the cuckoo pops out and calls ten times. At the last call—suddenly and indiscernibly—a secret door opens in the wall's upholstery. Lena comes out. Lena is a very beautiful young girl, dressed in a long white dress. She takes several steps into the room, suddenly sees Sand, emits a cry and collapses to the floor. A tremendous thunderclap*].

Curtain

ACT II

[*The curtain rises on the same scene: Lena kneeling on the floor, Sand bent over her.*]

LENA: Don't kill me, don't kill me! Please don't kill me!

SAND: What are you talking about? Who are you? Please get up! [*Tries to help her up, but she pulls away*].

LENA: Don't touch me! Don't kill me! Don't pull me! I'll go myself! My God! My God! [*Thunder*]. It's an air raid! They're bombing us! They'll come and liberate me. If they come—when they come—I'll tell them you didn't touch me. They won't do anything to you, I'll ask them... don't kill me!

SAND: But what are you talking about, child! Who wants to kill you? [*Thunder*].

LENA: They're bombing!

SAND: Who's bombing? It's only thunder. A storm. Listen! Nobody's bombing. It's thunder! [*Lena listens a moment to distant thunder and is silent*].

LENA: I'm not Jewish. I... I'm the mistress of the castle. I'm not Jewish. You can ask the Count...

SAND: But I am Jewish.

LENA: [*Raises her head and looks at him*]. Maybe—you—really are Jewish. Do you want to hide? Come, I'll hide you... I'll show you the place. The Count will agree. He's hidden Jews here before. They won't find you.

SAND: Hide from whom? I didn't come here to hide. [*Pause*]. I'll go call Zabrodsky: Wait, I'll be right back.

LENA: Don't call him. He's not to blame. He saved me. And now *they* are sitting in his room downstairs. They'll murder you both—they'll murder the three of us…

SAND: Who will?

LENA: The officers—the generals—the Nazis…

SAND: Listen, child… I'm a librarian… I'm from Palestine… Nobody will hurt you. Listen carefully to what I'm saying: There are no Nazis now, no German generals. I came here to look for Jewish books… I… nobody wants to harm you… The war is over.

LENA: You were sent to me—they sent you. You're their accomplice; I know, there are Jews who work for them… Why did you wind the clock? Why did you call me? You know the secret!

SAND: Good heavens! I've already told you: the war's over. It ended a long, long time ago. There's no more war. We defeated the Nazis. Do you understand what I'm saying to you? [*She doesn't answer*]. Is there a doctor who looks after you?

LENA: You think I'm crazy? My God! Ah! I'm not crazy! But he says… I've been living here three years… and all the time—war. And if they find me, they'll kill me. They exterminate all the Jews. I've seen them do it…!

SAND: But there are no Nazis here… [*Completely at a loss, Sand stands over her, looking at her; suddenly he remembers—he pulls out a newspaper from his pocket*]. Here! [*Offers her the paper*]. Read it, it's today's paper. Take it.

LENA: [*Makes no move to take the paper*]. I don't want to. Don't touch me! [*Grasps the black ribbon around her neck*]. You'll never get a chance to abuse me. No, never!

SAND: [*Handing her the paper*]. Do you know how to read?

LENA: What do you want from me?… I know how…

SAND: But if you read the papers, you must know the war's over…

LENA: I don't read newspapers. I haven't read any, for three years…

[*Cautiously extends her hand to the newspaper as if afraid it will scorch her*].

SAND: Here, take it. What are you afraid of? Take it, it's today's paper. [*Sees that she's eyeing the paper*]. Here! Look; here's the date.

LENA: [*Finally takes the paper*]. The date's correct. I wrote the date on the wall. Every day, for three years…

SAND: On the wall?

LENA: [*Doesn't answer. Sitting on the floor, she begins reading, frightened yet transfixed. Sand stands above her, watching her. Finally she looks up at him*]. I don't understand… I don't understand it!

SAND: But this is no way to read! Get up, sit over here, and read this through! [*She goes over to the sofa*].

SAND: There's not enough light here. Wait a moment, I'll put on the light—it'll be easier for you to read.

LENA: [*By the sofa*]. Don't put on the light! Don't put it on. They'll see. They never go very far. They might see the light through a crack.

SAND: But there's nobody around here. No Nazis, don't you understand? You can put on the lights and open all the windows…

LENA: Don't put on the light! Don't open the windows.

SAND: All right, I won't. Can you read in this light?

LENA: Yes… [*Sits down on the sofa, begins reading*].

SAND: [*Stands and observes her*].

LENA: This is a real newspaper?

SAND: Here, have a good look at me—do I look like someone who means harm to you?

LENA: [*Continues looking at the headlines. Turns the paper over, reads a bit, then drops it to the floor*]. Tell me, tell me, is this a real paper?

SAND: This is a newspaper which I bought this morning in the capital, and yesterday I bought a newspaper just like this one and the day before yesterday and a week ago. Everybody in this country reads this paper—except for you, maybe…

LENA: [*Looking at him with bewildered eyes*]. Yes! Yes! Ah—this… but he didn't tell me! Good God, he didn't tell me! He never said anything! [*Buries her face in her hands, sits rigidly*].

SAND: [*Goes over the left door, opens it slightly and calls out quietly*]. Dora! Dora!

DORA: [*Comes in. She had begun to undress and now she buttons up her blouse again*]. What happened? I thought I heard a scream?

SAND: Come here!

DORA: I thought I was imagining things. There was thunder... and my nerves tonight... but what...

SAND: [*Points to* LENA]. Here—You must help me—you must do something!

DORA: Who is she? Where did she come from?

SAND: A secret door opened, in the wall, I think, I don't know who she is.

DORA: [*Puts on all the lights—to have a good look at* LENA].

LENA: Ah...! Now they'll see! Now they'll come! You...

SAND: Calm down, child... you needn't be afraid of light any more. [LENA *buries her face in her hands again.* SAND *whispers something to* DORA, *of which only the last words are heard*]. And maybe...

DORA: She's not sane?

LENA: I am sane! But now—I don't know...

SAND: She claims Zabrodsky saved her...

LENA: He did! Yes, he saved me...

SAND: [*Making a gesture of despair*]. You talk to her. In the meantime I'll call Zabrodsky—I didn't want to leave her alone—now I'll call him, maybe he can explain the whole thing.

LENA: No! No! Don't call him! Don't go to him! No, no!

SAND: All right, I won't call him. [*Steps aside*].

DORA: [*Goes over to the sofa; to* LENA]. May I sit down next to you? [LENA *doesn't answer,* DORA *sits down*]. You're so pale! [*Silence*]. I can see you haven't been out in the sun for a long time! Don't you ever go out?

LENA: [*Shakes her head no*].

DORA: What a pity! The days have been so lovely! The sun was out even this morning. I didn't think there'd be a storm!

LENA: A storm?

DORA: Didn't you hear the thunder? [LENA *doesn't answer*].

SAND: She thought it was an air raid.

DORA: Air raid? But there haven't been any air raids for over two years. You thought the war was still going on?

LENA: The war...

DORA: [*Picks up the newspaper from the floor*]. But there's no war! The war's over. Have you read the paper?

LENA: Yes.

DORA: Well, then you know there's no war! I understand, you were closed up here and didn't go out... maybe you didn't meet people and they didn't tell you? Is that so?

LENA: Yes...

DORA: Now, then, as soon as the storm is over we'll go outside... don't you be afraid, we'll go out with you. Tomorrow morning will be a beautiful day and you'll see for yourself. Yes? [LENA *doesn't answer*].

DORA: We came from Palestine—and I've met lots of young people here who are still afraid of the war. But now they're not afraid any more. They go out, wherever they please, for walks, to the theater, to the cinema... do you understand what I'm saying?

LENA: Yes.

DORA: [*Shows her the newspaper*]. Here, you see: It says here... but you read it yourself. Well, then, let's get acquainted: my name's Dora, what's yours?

LENA: It's a real paper? There's really no war now? No Nazis? It's a real paper? Tell me! Is that true?

DORA: It's true, dear. The war's been over for a long time. Hitler was killed, the Nazis defeated. That's why we're here, he and I. We're both Jews. Don't you see: We're free and we're not afraid.

LENA: And this newspaper was... there are—newspapers like this now?

DORA: Yes, but who are you?

LENA: And who are you? Why did the Count let you into the castle? Why did you wind the clock? Why did you call me? Why did you bring me out? Why did you wind the clock?

DORA: What clock?

SAND: When you left, I climbed up this ladder to have a good look at the clock.

LENA: Yes, the clock… this clock.

SAND: I opened it and found a key inside. I wound it up and it rang…

LENA: Ten times. That's the signal.

SAND: What signal?

LENA: For me—to come out. It means there are no Nazis here—that I can come out.

SAND: [*To* DORA]. And then she appeared. It was all so quick and unexpected, I didn't even see how it happened. But there she was—all of a sudden.

LENA: Because that's the signal between us.

DORA: Between who?

LENA: Between me and the Count.

SAND: I didn't know anything about this signal. I'm a watchmaker's son and I like clocks… I was just tinkering and the cuckoo…

LENA: But where did you come from?

DORA: We're from Palestine, both of us. You know where that is?

LENA: Yes.

DORA: [*To* SAND]. She's Jewish?

SAND: Yes, of course…

DORA: Are you from here? From these parts or from the city?

LENA: From the city. It's far… I think it's very far away.

DORA: Yes, it's far. And you came here on foot?

LENA: Yes.

DORA: During the war? You ran away?

LENA: Yes.

DORA: And you found shelter here?

LENA: Yes… here—shelter…

DORA: And do you have anyone? Are any of your family still alive?

LENA: Why are you questioning me? Questions, questions, questions! I have no one, no one!

DORA: If you don't want to answer, you don't have to. Nobody will force you. But I thought you wanted us to help you.

LENA: But who are you? Yes, who are you? That's what you don't want to tell me!

DORA: I do, very much. Look here—this man—his name is Michael Sand. He's a librarian and he was sent here to look for books—after the war... [*Sees that Lena is not convinced by this. To* SAND]. Show her your papers, Sand! [SAND *hesitates*]. Yes, yes, show her. And also the Palestinian passport! [SAND *gives the documents to* DORA, *who hands them over to* LENA]. You can sit down and examine them, take your time and read them through. [LENA *takes the papers—looks at them and at* SAND *by turns*].

DORA: [*To* SAND]. She came out of a secret door, you said?

SAND: Yes, I think so... from there. [*Points at the tapestry.* DORA *is about to go over there, but at that very moment* LENA *hands back the papers.* DORA *goes over to her and takes them*]. Well, did you have a look?

LENA: Yes.

DORA: And my name is Dr. Ringel, Dora Ringel. I work for an organization called "Youth Aliya." Of course, you don't know what that is.

LENA: I do... before... when I was a child... people from Palestine used to come out to our house... my father was... my father knew those people...

DORA: Excellent! Then I don't have to explain to you.... You know, it's quite possible that I knew your father. And even you too, when you were a child. What's your last name?

LENA: [*Doesn't answer*].

DORA: [*Doesn't repeat the question, sensing that it is premature*]. And you've been here a long time?

LENA: Yes, a long time... but how did *you* come here?

DORA: I've shown you the papers. He's looking for books here... and I came along to see the castle. And because of the storm, we stayed on for the night. Now, is that clear?

LENA: Storm? [*Listens*]. It's quiet now. They're not bombing any more. Why did they stop bombing the moment you came here?

DORA: But listen…

LENA: You put on the light and that was the signal and they stopped the bombing…

SAND: But can't you understand, child, there was no bombing. You know yourself that there are no more bombings…

LENA: Yes, but what was it? I heard explosions.

SAND: There was a storm, thunder and lightning…

LENA: [*As if to herself*]. A storm… thunder and lightning… and behold a pale horse and his name that sat on him was death… yes… [*As if awakening*]. A storm? There was just a storm outside?

DORA: Yes.

LENA: [*Listening*]. And now the storm is over. And the rain has stopped. There's no more rain.

SAND: [*Listening*]. Yes.

LENA: And where's the Count?

SAND: Probably in his room, below. Do you want to see him?

DORA: Sand!

LENA: No, no, no! I don't want to. He didn't hear the clock?

SAND: I don't know. I don't think so. There was a storm.

LENA: You can't hear the cuckoo downstairs… unless you listen very carefully—very carefully. He told me.

DORA: But who are you? How did you get here?

LENA: You came here to interrogate me… yes, yes, now I know. You won't get a single word out of me! You want to find out about me and the Count! But I won't tell you. I won't talk, you can kill me. I won't talk!

DORA: You don't have to. Nobody will force you to say anything, if you don't feel like it. But now you know all about us. And you know, you know just as well as we do, there's no war any more.

LENA: I don't know anything. Newspapers and documents can be forged. Everything is possible, the Nazis know everything, they have friends…

SAND: There are no Nazis any more.

DORA: Look, the storm is over, go and open the window, look out and see how quiet everything is, there's no war.

LENA: Don't touch the windows! It's forbidden! It's forbidden, they'll see…

DORA: My God, what have they done to this girl, who did this to her?! Don't you believe us? I'll tell you what: We'll turn out the light and shut our eyes, and then you can disappear just the way you came. We won't even know where you've gone to.

SAND: Or else you can leave, you can go to Count Zabrodsky and tell him we're here. You're free to do as you please, absolutely free. Well, tell us what we're supposed to do, order us out of here—and we'll go.

LENA: No! No! Don't go, I'm afraid now! I'm afraid to stay by myself, without you… I'm even afraid of the Count now.

SAND: All right, if you want us to, we'll stay and help you. But we don't even know who you are.

LENA: My name's Lena.

DORA: And how did you get here?

LENA: How did I get here? Ah, I didn't know anything… I thought…

DORA: Did they torture you here?

LENA: Torture? Me?—They didn't even know I was here. And he was good to me, he was so good to me! He did everything… He took wonderful care of me… there, below, in my secret room…. I had everything I needed. He brought me every-thing… himself… good food… at first, when I was hungry and couldn't eat like everybody, he used to come down and feed me with a spoon, like a baby…. I was sick then, too… and afterwards, he brought me beautiful dresses, and I also had books down there, I still have them—now. Only it's for-bidden to open the windows… yes, they might see. And at night—I am the mistress of the castle, and everything, every-thing is mine… when the Nazis aren't here.

DORA: But there have been no Nazis for a long time, for over two years.

LENA: Ah, yes, yes…

DORA: But, how did you get here?

LENA: When the Nazis came… that is, they'd been in the country a long time before that—but when they came to our house… I ran away. At first I hid in the house and then I ran away—I don't know how. They took father and mother—and little Zoska and Paul—and I ran away. I hid in a forest for a few days—and at night—I walked—I walked and walked and sometimes I sang…

SAND: You sang?!

LENA: Yes… yes… quietly… they didn't hear… it doesn't matter… and one night I didn't have any strength left—and I came here—I collapsed here… He came out with the Nazis who lived here—he hates them… he really hates them! And I was hungry and exhausted… he brought me in—he risked his life for my sake—but he took me in—he hid me here, in this secret room—he saved my life and gave me everything… everything… and he… [*Silence*].

DORA: [*Witheringly*]. And afterwards—when victory came—and the Nazis were taken captive—he didn't tell you? [*Silence. To* SAND]. What a low trick!

LENA: [*Rises. With sudden fury*]. I'll go! I don't want to talk to you! How can you speak that way about the Count? How do you dare? He saved me! *He* did!

SAND: [*Stopping her*]. Please, sit down.

LENA: [*Goes back and sits down, exhausted*]. Ah, what do I care now!

DORA: But don't you understand: he deceived you.

LENA: He—loves—me.

DORA: And you—him?

LENA: [*Doesn't answer*].

DORA: If you loved him—there would be no need to hold you here in constant fear of a war that's over—you could remain of your own free will, because of your love, nobody would force you to leave him. Do you understand? [*Silence*].

DORA: How old are you?

LENA: Nineteen… and a half…

DORA: And a half? [DORA *and* SAND *exchange glances*].

LENA: It's not his fault... I told him the truth. Yes, yes! I said that when the war was over, I'd go away. Maybe I shouldn't have told him that—but I dreamt, oh I dreamt all the time, that I would be able to walk outside, free as a bird, in the sun, in the open air... to go and walk—when the war was over...

DORA: Well, the war *is* over. You're free. You can go anywhere and do whatever you like.

LENA: No.

DORA: Why?

LENA: When you dream—it's different. He used to say that the war would never come to an end. That one day they'd discover us and kill us. He wanted us both to die on the same day, together. And I wanted to live. He said that the fourth kingdom would come after death—the fourth kingdom! Do you know what that is?

SAND: Have you become a Christian?

LENA: No. The Count says, there's no difference between Jew and Christian. He says it's not important. He believes only in the fourth kingdom.

SAND: What is that?

LENA: The fourth kingdom? [SAND *nods*]. There will be no living and dead there, no young and old. There will be a great love there and eternal grandeur, and he that overcometh shall not be hurt of the second death... and everything will be as it once was—only different! Oh, I don't know... in my heart I wanted a simple life, like the one I once had. Yes, just an ordinary life. But now... everything was a lie. I don't want anything.

DORA: Now you can leave this place.

LENA: Where will I go? To whom? They murdered father and mother and the children. He's the only one in the whole world who loves me. [*Passionately*]. His love made him deceive me! He really loves me! I knew it, I knew it even before he told me. I pitied him so much. I told him first that I loved him... It's my fault... I wanted to have somebody... sitting there by myself in the secret room—and the windows shut all the time, and you can't even peek outside. He was so wonderful to me and so unhappy… and everything all together…. I never saw people like that before… ah, it's not that, I don't know, maybe I deceived him. Yes, of course, I deceived him even more, I didn't tell him the truth—not about loving him—I don't know about that—but the other thing… yes, yes, I never told him that if we'd have to die—I wouldn't die like him—I wouldn't let them torture me—I never told him that I have… [*Suddenly, her hand gripping the black ribbon around her throat, she stops short*]. Ah, what am I saying! What do you want from me? It doesn't matter!

DORA: But how did you live here all the time?

LENA: At night, when there was no danger, he used to wind the clock, always at ten, and I would come out to him. I would be the mistress of the castle. He looked after me as if I was a small daughter. He read lovely books with me, and taught me things that I didn't have a chance to learn in school. Much more beautiful than those they teach in school. Sometimes he would read me the Revelation, about the end of the world and the resurrection… and he used to sit with me in the music room… have you been there?

SAND: Yes.

LENA: …and play to me. He plays like an angel. He plays Chopin for me.

DORA: [*Mockingly*]. Chopin! Just what I thought!

LENA: No, no. You mustn't talk that way about him. He plays like an angel… ah, you don't know. Sometimes, when I wasn't afraid… when the Nazis would go for a long time… that is… well, yes, when he said that the Nazis were gone, we would even dance a little. [*To* DORA]. Do you waltz?

DORA: Then you want to stay on here. To waltz, to be the mistress of the castle at night—and during the day he isn't even the owner any more. They confiscated it and nationalized it—and now he—your Count—is only the caretaker of the castle—

you should know that. And you want to listen to Chopin, to read books about the end of the world, to be bound to a man—who deceived you… to live with him until he dies and rots—and then what?

LENA: I don't know. I don't want to live that way. I don't want to live at all any more… I want to die. Why did you come here? Who asked you to come?

DORA: We're here, and we're going to help you leave this place. You'll come with us to Palestine. You'll join a group your own age. You'll live, work, you'll be healthy and free and happy like all the other young people.

LENA: No.

SAND: You still don't believe us?

LENA: I believe you. But… what's the good of it? I'm already… what will I do there with young people? I'm impure!

DORA: [*Looks at* SAND. *To* LENA]. You know, in this war, lots of young girls had much more horrible experiences.

LENA: I don't know anything about other girls. I'm impure!

DORA: [*To* SAND]. Well, what do you say?

SAND: [*Begins laughing, good-naturedly—but both women look at him almost in fright*] Well, what can you do about it? All young girls like to use such pretty words. My little niece, when she had her fifth birthday, announced to me, with great jubilation, just like Lena did now: "Uncle Mike, you know, I'm now a woman with a past!"

LENA: [*Laughs*].

SAND: So, you see, you'll find there another woman with a past. And believe me… [*Lena's laughter turns into crying*].

SAND: You're crying? Good, cry it out. It'll do you good. [*She calms down slowly*]. That's enough. You've cried and that's that. Give me your hand, lady with a past. You're not mad at me? [*He extends his hand and she touches it hesitantly*]. No. Not this way. A good squeeze. That's right! That's good, isn't it?

LENA: [*Smiling through her tears*]. Yes.

DORA: [*Patting her head*]. Here… you're smiling. That's nice. And now, calm down, dear, calm down… [*As she talks and pats her head she notices an amulet suspended from the black velvet ribbon about her neck*].

DORA: [*Panicky, holding on the amulet*]. What's this?

LENA: This… nothing at all. It's an amulet my mother gave me.

DORA: [*Without letting go*]. No. You tell me what this is.

LENA: Leave me alone! I told you: an amulet. Against the evil eye. My mother gave it to me when I was a child.

DORA: You give that to me right now, do you hear?! [*To* SAND]. Do you know what she has there?—Poison! They used to keep it in amulets like this: Those Jews who succeeded in getting poison. Much good it did them: The Nazis usually found it right away when they searched for valuables. But there were those who managed to swallow it—when they had no choice… in those days it was… yes! but now you don't need it. Do you hear?

LENA: [*Doesn't answer*].

DORA: You give that to me right now! But right this very minute without another word! Do you hear!

LENA: My God! What do you want from me? I won't give it to you! I won't… It was the only thing I had left. Mother gave it to me, mother said that maybe I'd need it… this was my secret… even the Count didn't know. I deceived him! Yes. Yes. Yes!!! I deceived him. I've already told you that. He didn't know, that if the Nazis came to kill us, I wouldn't die at their hands, like him. I… I didn't want them to abuse me… I didn't want them to torture me. And I had a way out… only for me and not for him… I didn't tell him… ah, I didn't tell him—not only because of the Nazis—sometimes I thought I wouldn't be able to bear this life any longer and then… ah, what am I telling you… now you come…

DORA: But understand, Lena, try to understand: now it's all over. Now you don't need it any more, you don't need it at all.

LENA: [*Doesn't answer*].

DORA: [*To Sand*]. Maybe you'll…

SAND: [*Who has walked away a bit, comes closer to Lena*].

LENA: [*Kneeling*]. Don't take it from me! No! Please! Don't take it.

DORA: Hush... he'll hear you...

LENA: [*In a lower voice; she's used to controlling her voice under stress*]. No! Don't take it! Don't take it!

SAND: [*Closing in*]. Lena!

LENA: I won't give it up! It's mine. Mother gave this to me. It's the last thing. The last way out...

SAND: But Lena...

LENA: No, no, no! I won't give it to you... you're strong... you can take it by force... but you'd better kill me...

SAND: I won't take anything from you by force. But you'll give it to me yourself. Of your own free will. Right now!

LENA: I won't give it. No!! You come and take everything. You take my life and the Count and everything I had.... You take away my freedom, to live or to die... you...

SAND: But understand... [*Suddenly changes his mind*]. You're right Lena. [*To* DORA, *who motions to him that he should trick Lena and take away the poison*]. No, leave her alone... [*To* LENA]. We meant to help you, Lena. But... calm down, come sit here... from now on nobody will take anything from you by force. You're absolutely free. You're free even to die, if you choose death. To live or to die—any time *you* make the choice. [*Tries to help her up, but she avoids him*]. Don't you believe me? There's no trickery here, Lena. I swear to you by everything that's holy to me: We won't take anything away from you, we won't force you to do anything against your will. I swear to you! Now, get up! [*Lifts her up carefully; completely spent, she lets him seat her*].

DORA: In the end, Lena, you'll see that you yourself will give us the poison. Why? Now you want to live, to live and not to die. You still have no idea how much you want to live... but you want to, don't you?

LENA: I don't know.

DORA: You must want *life*, you must want it very badly, and then...

LENA: What then? What good is it? I don't have anybody in the world. No one at all. There was the Count, but now… I don't have a living soul in the whole world.

DORA: How can you be so sure?

LENA: I know. I know they took father and mother and the children…

DORA: That was your entire family?

LENA: There were others… but what's the use, they're probably all dead. I have no one.

DORA: What's your last name, Lena? [LENA *is silent*].

DORA: I asked you what your last name was?

LENA: [*Bursting out*]. Oh, what a fool I am, what a fool! You sit there and get all the information out of me! You want to know everything, all their names, and how it happened, and everything! Why did I open my mouth! Why did I trust you? Why did I believe all your lies? Now I know that the Nazis sent you. I've told you everything about me and the Count… and now only this last detail is missing, maybe somebody is still alive—that's what you want to know!

SAND: But you know very well that now you're talking nonsense. You've gone through the newspaper!

LENA: Newspaper! How do I know your newspaper isn't forged?! Why is all this going on without the Count? Why should I believe you more than him? I've known him for three years, he's been good to me, he saved me! He hates the Nazis! And you… who are you! Where's the Count? Where is he right now? Tell me, why don't you answer?

SAND: I've already told you, he's downstairs, in his room.

LENA: Yes, you told me! And fool that I am, I believed you! But you've already taken him! You've handed him over to the Nazis! They're torturing him. Maybe they've murdered him?…

SAND: You can go down and see for yourself if he's there.

LENA: [*As if threatening them*]. I will. I'll go down and call him.

DORA: Go right ahead, you're free to do whatever you please.

LENA: That's what you say!

DORA: Well, find out. Go and call him. Why aren't you going? [*A taut silence. After great hesitation,* LENA *rises and goes to right door. She exits. Pause*].

DORA: There you are. She's really gone!

SAND: Very good.

DORA: What's so "very good"?

SAND: Very good that she's decided to do something. You know yourself that was necessary!

DORA: Oh, please! She's gone—down these steps, with the poison! What will become of her! Go call her!

SAND: I will not. Let her do what she pleases.

DORA: But she... with the poison...

SAND: Nothing's going to happen: She really wants to live now more than she knows.

DORA: Oh, you're so sure of yourself! And now she'll really call him! That criminal!

SAND: Oh, now he's a criminal!

DORA: Well, isn't he? Or is this part of that refined culture that charms you out of your wits? Huh? That wonderful tradition! That noble class of delicate souls! Now you see how harmless they are—there's no need to argue with them any more! Ah!

SAND: There's no need to argue—about abstractions, and in general, my dear, you exaggerate!

DORA: What do I exaggerate! Where do I exaggerate! Didn't you see what he did to her, to his poor girl? Ah! Last week I had a similar case with a Father Superior and a boy! But I could still understand that... when people want to continue educating a child in their religion... or when a family that adopted children becomes attached to them... but this!

SAND: This you can't understand?

DORA: I can't and I don't want to!

SAND: The main thing is—that you don't want to. A man whose world has fallen to pieces! A man who fought with courage and devotion—for a world that isn't his. And then he found something in this world, one human being that he could love... All right, I'm not justifying what he did, just as I don't justify your Father Superior. But I can understand—and I *want* to understand—his weakness. Don't you see, it's just an ordinary erotic relationship, the love of an old man for a young girl—this is the straw he's clinging to in an imaginary world, which is dearer to him than anything else! Why she—she's not an ordinary girl for him—she's the Lady of the Castle!

DORA: Lady of the Castle! The devil take all your philosophy! I'm only capable of seeing things the way they are, and that's how I want to see them… and that's the way they really are, yes! Ah—I'm getting all mixed up myself—this—this is such a—it's not real…

SAND: It is real, Dora. Reality has many faces, some of which are very strange…

DORA: But she'll call him! She'll call him now. That horrible man… and the whole thing will start all over again. You don't… but I… I'm afraid of him!

SAND: In any event, we can't avoid meeting him. We all have to leave this place and he has the keys.

DORA: We'll have to find another way out.

SAND: There's no other way.

DORA: Maybe there's an exit from her room?

SAND: I don't imagine he left her a way out of here!

DORA: There you are! And after all this you say he's not a criminal!

SAND: After all this, I think he's the most unfortunate man I've met in all these years!

DORA: Ah, I don't care about that! I want to save Lena. And I don't want to see him… she won't dare to leave if he's here.

SAND: Then we may have to leave her here for a while until she decides to go of her own free will.

DORA: Leave her here!? In this house? With that old man? And the poison? Ah, what… [*Listens attentively*]. There, there, there! Do you hear?

SAND: I don't hear anything. What's come over you?

DORA: Quiet! He's coming!

SAND: But she just went to call him…

DORA: [*Without paying attention to him*]. I can't stand it... I hear steps!

SAND: [*Listening*]. There are no steps, Dora. You're imagining things.

DORA: Imagining? Yes, maybe... maybe you're right. Why this whole business is inconceivable from the very beginning... How is it?...—a girl suddenly steps out of a wall at night! And this castle! And he—I'm almost ready to swear that I'm imagining things. That all this is a dream... that there's been nobody here besides us.... What a silence. Why, it's all impossible. Things like this happen only in dreams... in bad dreams... look... listen! Do you really hear my voice? Was she really here?

SAND: Take it easy Dora. What a sad business...

DORA: No. Was she really here?

SAND: But I saw her too...

DORA: Yes, yes, I know. I'm tired... and it's all so strange. Was she really here? [*The door opens and* LENA *comes in*].

SAND: Here she is.

DORA: [*Stares blankly, as if shaking off a dream*].

SAND: [*To* LENA]. Did you call him?

LENA: No.

DORA: Isn't he there?

LENA: I don't know... I... I went out of here... and then I started going down the steps. I've never been below... because there... I've never been there at all... only the first night—when he brought me in. I'm afraid to go down there. I can't.

DORA: [*Strengthened, making an effort*]. Maybe you want me to go down with you? You'll see, there's nothing to be afraid of.

LENA: No...no. I don't want to call him. I stood on the steps. I stood there and thought. Now I know: I'm not afraid of being with you. It was silly, what I said to you. I believe you.

DORA: That's wonderful, Lena. Is there anything you want?

LENA: I don't know. I don't want anything. Only talk to me some more. I haven't talked to anybody for so many years... except for the Count. You asked me something before, didn't you? What was it?

DORA: I asked for your last name. But if you don't want to, you don't have to answer.

LENA: My last name is Brabant.

SAND: What a strange name!

DORA: It's a name that sticks in your memory.

LENA: Memory! Now we have to remember everything. There's nothing left in the world except our memory. And we're—just tombstones. That's what the Count says... but don't call him!

DORA: [*As if she hadn't heard her*]. Tell me, Lena Brabant—I remember this name very well. Your parents had a jewelry shop near the museum?

LENA: Yes! You know that?

DORA: I grew up here. Most of the Jews here more or less knew each other.

LENA: And then you went to Palestine.

DORA: Yes.

LENA: [*Bitterly*]. You had an easy time of it, you were safe! You weren't persecuted, killed, tortured—what do you know about us! [SAND *wants to reply, but* DORA *silences him with a gesture*].

DORA: Was there a woman in your family by the name of Lisa Brabant?

LENA: Yes. My aunt. My father's younger sister.

DORA: We went to school together. Many years ago. Then she married a doctor. Sherman was his name, wasn't it?

LENA: Yes. Why are you talking about them? They're probably all dead.

DORA: No, Lisa is alive. Back home. In Palestine. Her husband and my husband work in the same hospital. Even Sand knows her. Why you know Lisa Sherman, Sand!

SAND: Yes.

LENA: [*As if figuring out something*]. You might see her sometime? Then, please, please tell her, that I sang the song and that helped me.

294

SAND: What song?

LENA: She'll know… [*To* DORA]. You went to school with her? Maybe you know the song too?

DORA: What song?

LENA: Ah, I keep on talking this way and you… you don't understand what I mean. But I can explain everything. I'm completely sane. It's this way. When I was little I used to be afraid of the dark. And then Aunt Lisa taught me a song. Just a children's song. She said that when you sing it in the dark, the fear goes away. And best of all, is to sing the song while walking. It's a simple children's song—you know—you've probably also heard it. It goes like this. [*Begins to walk the room and sing, as children do*].

> Rooster, rooster
> With your comb so fine,
> Cry out, cry out
> And the sun will shine.
> Cry out, cry out
> And that Lord of mine
> Will chase away the dark
> And the sun will shine.

You know this song?

DORA: Yes, we sang it when we were children.

LENA: Lisa taught me to sing it. And I—that night—when I ran away to the forest, I was no longer a child—but it was such a horror! I don't know how to pray… I ran by myself in the night, in the dark, it's a good thing it was dark, because in the light it's easier to find those who run away… but I was afraid not only of the Nazis, but also of the dark, and so I ran all by myself in the forest and sang in a low voice: "Rooster, rooster, with your comb so fine"… and that helped me a bit… [*To* SAND]. When you see Aunt Lisa, tell her I'm thankful for the song.

SAND: I will.

DORA: You'll tell her this whole story yourself.

LENA: How do you mean?

DORA: Well, I've told you that Lisa is in Palestine. You'll come there with me. You'll go over to Lisa and tell her everything yourself.

LENA: Me?

DORA: Of course! I told you…

LENA: [*To* SAND]. You'll tell her. And if you don't feel like it, don't tell her. I don't care. They got away, they're alive there! And I was here—I could've died, I could've been murdered—what do they care…

DORA: But how do you know? Maybe they looked for you? Who could have guessed that you're still alive? After looking in vain for a long time, she was probably sure that you'd been killed with your family.

LENA: [*To* SAND]. She looked for me? She asked about me? She did something? You tell me. You. You always tell the truth. I know!

SAND: I don't know. I don't know her very well. We always spoke very little, and about other things.

LENA: Other things! They didn't even try to find me. But they're right, they're right…. Why look for me! The Count, he knows—he said we're already dead anyhow, that no one dies twice. And to come to life in the world of those who haven't even died once—that we can't do!

DORA: What has this man done to you! He's dead, he's a corpse. That's the truth. He belongs to the world of the dead. But you, a young, healthy, lovely girl—all of life is still ahead of you. How many times have I seen people who went through worse horrors, who were sick, broken, wounded, dehumanized. And you should come with me if only to see them now. With what happiness, with what a lust for happiness, they've begun to live again like human beings. And they really had no one in the world—not one living soul—but at your age it's not so difficult to start again. If you only saw them…

LENA: Maybe the others can—I can't. No. Maybe the others don't know what I know.

DORA: What do you know?

LENA: [*Suddenly as if in a dream*]. I know, that I was really dead. I know that I have no way back to the living. Only he who was faithful unto death was given the crown of life. I know that physical death is only one stage—a getaway to the fourth kingdom!

SAND: Again the fourth kingdom!

LENA: In the fourth kingdom there are no dead and no living. No young and no old. He who has overcome death while alive, shall enter the fourth kingdom. And he that overcometh shall not be hurt of the second death...

DORA: Do you really believe this?

LENA: [*Pensive, as if coming out of a dream, trying to answer honestly*]. Sometimes yes, sometimes no. When I dreamt of life by myself—secretly, without knowing then I dreamt otherwise. Then I didn't believe. But when there was no more hope, when I knew I would die, when I knew that one way or the other—it was sure death, then the Count gave me this dream. And this was my own dream. I dreamt it—when hope was gone... and I believed... why did you come here? This was the last dream!

SAND: But that was a dream of hopelessness, Lena. Now you have more than hope. You have life itself.

LENA: But I love my dreams.

DORA: And do you think that people who are alive and free have no dreams? Do you think that in our world—his and mine—people don't dream? Before you came here, didn't you have dreams you loved?

LENA: Then... yes... but everything was different then...

DORA: Right, and now everything will be different again... it may not be so easy in the beginning, Lena, it may not be so simple, but.... Do you still remember something of your life before you came here? Didn't you yourself say that you wanted to walk freely outside? Do you remember what that is, how it felt?

LENA: I think… I do… to walk outside…

DORA: But to walk outside you've got to leave this place. First of all you've got to get out of here.

LENA: Yes… to get out of here…

DORA: And to do some other very simple things, that everybody does, but you've already forgotten how they're done.

LENA: What?

DORA: Well, for instance, to work, to meet people—or… here— you can't walk in town in these shoes. You're used to having everything brought to you, done for you.—But tomorrow, when we leave this place—you'll have to go into a shop to buy shoes.

LENA: But I have no money!

DORA: Here, you see! That will also be one of the problems—later on. But in the meantime we'll give you… and then—we'll have to take care of that too.

LENA: [*Looks at Dora's shoes*]. That's what they wear—now?

DORA: Yes…

LENA: You bought them?

DORA: [*Laughing*]. Naturally!

LENA: You—simply stepped into a store and said, "Give me a pair of shoes" and picked them out.

DORA: One night last week, I was taking a walk and I passed a show window…

LENA: At night! In a show window!

DORA: Yes…

LENA: At night, in the street!

DORA: Yes. What's so surprising?

LENA: The windows are lit up? There's light in the streets at night? And lamps? You're allowed to switch them on?

DORA: Yes, yes, of course!

LENA: In a lighted street… I've forgotten. It's been so long… And during the day?

DORA: What, during the day?

LENA: I haven't seen the sun… nor the moon. Not even the moon—

all these years… only a bit—in this window… here… but it
was closed.

DORA: You see! Such simple things! That everybody takes for granted!
And you'll see them; the sun, and the show windows and the
moon. You can even see the moon right now—is the moon
out tonight, Sand?

SAND: Yes.

DORA: All we have to do is open the window…

LENA: No… and in the daytime—lots of people walk in the streets?

DORA: Yes, Lena, the streets are packed with people. They leave their
homes, go into restaurants, just walk around… Do you want
to walk in the street, in the sun?

LENA: Yes, and when the rain comes down… [*Suddenly*]. But I
don't want to see them always! No, I don't want to see them.
Always—the same…

DORA: See who?

LENA: Those who were here before… They knew father and mother.
They let them be killed. I know, they walk the streets, all of
them—even our neighbors, I don't want to!

DORA: But you won't see them. We'll go far away from here. We
won't stay in this country.

LENA: Ah, yes, yes… I forgot. [*To* SAND]. Far away, yes, and never—
you'll take me away from here? Won't you?

SAND: Yes, Lena.

LENA: And the Count?

DORA: What about the Count?

LENA: He'll stay on here? Always by himself? Always closed up?

DORA: But understand, Lena! He wasn't closed up here all these
years! *He* went outside, breathed the fresh air, walked the
streets. He only told *you* that it's forbidden to go out and see
the sun.

LENA: There—I know—there's lots of light and sun. I want to go out.
I want so much to go out!

DORA: Well, then…

LENA: But the Count—he'll stay here.

DORA: Again the Count!

LENA: Again, again, again! Don't look at me that way! You don't know. [*Points at Sand*]. He knows... I don't know why, but he knows!!—Ah, when we were locked up here—and death surrounded us. Death!—No. I don't love him—don't look at me that way!! Maybe I... he was the only living soul! I want to go—but I can't. I can't.

SAND: Lena, listen—I'll tell you something—something—that can't be put into words. I know it's hard for you. I know you're sorry for the Count. And you're right—I do understand. I'm also sorry for him. Very sorry. But you've got to go. You understand—you mustn't stay here! I can't explain it. But you know that you've got to go. You must live. You must live free—without him. What went on here—is finished. You understand, Lena?

LENA: Yes, yes, I understand. I—I want to go somewhere else, to another country, far away... and not to come back... ever...

DORA: Then you're coming with us! And the best thing would be to leave right away. [*In a practical manner*]. But you can't go like this. Do you have any clothes down in your room?

LENA: [*Mechanically—her thoughts are elsewhere*]. Yes.

DORA: Could you go down quickly and get dressed?

LENA: [*Doesn't answer*].

DORA: Hurry up, Lena, hurry up and get dressed!

LENA: [*Unhesitatingly*]. I'm staying here.

[*Silence. After a long pause, the cuckoo pops out of the clock. Eleven. Immediately after this Zabrodsky bursts into the room*].

Curtain

ACT III

[*The curtain rises on the same scene: Zabrodsky standing at some distance from Lena.*]

ZABRODSKY: [*To* LENA]. Well, the war is over, Lena.

DORA: It was over two years ago.

ZABRODSKY: The war is over, Lena. You are free, you can leave.

DORA: The war has been over for more than two years. Two years of lost freedom! If you hadn't...

ZABRODSKY: Do you hear, Lena, you could have been free two years ago, even more than two years ago. You could have been living in this earthly paradise of theirs. You could have wandered with refugee convoys, looked for work, struggled with hunger, filth, ugliness until you dropped... and instead you were held captive here, you wasted the best years of your life on an old man...

DORA: Who deceived you for two years.

ZABRODSKY: [*Now almost out of his mind*]. Who deceived you for two years. The others do it much more quickly. They are known as honest people. They come to your house under false pretenses, tell you a story about a search for books, spy on you, wind the clock and deceive two people...

SAND: We didn't spy on you, we knew nothing about your secrets. I just happened to wind the clock...

DORA: He'll soon say we also engineered the storm...

SAND: Mr. Zabrodsky, I don't know what you've been through, I don't know what made you do such a thing—I'm trying to understand...

ZABRODSKY: [*Disdainfully*]. My good sir! Don't bother! We shall never understand each other. [*To* LENA]. Well, Lena, you are free to do as you wish: you may even help them hand me over to the police, you may testify against me... after all, if it were not for me...

LENA: [*Keeps quiet*].

SAND: [*With sudden understanding*]. You know very well, Count, that she won't do that. You saved her life… only let her leave in peace.

ZABRODSKY: Do you hear that, Lena? Such exemplary generosity! You may leave in peace, Lena.

DORA: What's all this talking about, all these fine phrases and stratagems? She has eyes to see!

LENA: [*Keeps quiet*].

ZABRODSKY: She has eyes to see… Surely you see what I have done to you! Why are you silent? Tell them, *you* tell them everything you have against me… [*Burying his face in his hands*]. … for if I should tell them, who would believe me? If I should tell the true story of my life—if I should say that I have never deceived anyone [*Now, without sensing it, he turns to Sand*] that I have never violated the honor of a woman, that it has never occurred to me to seduce a girl, that I have never done a dishonest deed… yes! Who would believe me! Who would believe me that when I saw this poor creature running and stumbling in the forest, I did not for one moment think of myself; when I brought her in, carrying her in my arms, the castle was full of armed Nazis—who would believe that in those days I did not even have a good look at her face, because I was afraid to put on the light even in the secret room! And all those days, guarding her here like a precious stone—I had no idea what she looked like—I neither had the time nor the inclination to wonder whether she was beautiful or not; and who, who would believe me, an old man, already half-dead, that this began—and it was not only my doing… I was not alone in this…

LENA: [*Nods her head yes. Silence*].

ZABRODSKY: …and this began while they were still here in the house, and this meant everything to me—everything, everything… and afterwards… If I have wronged you, Lena, I must answer to God—only He shall judge me… [*To* SAND]. Do you know what that is, an old man's fear of losing everything…

SAND: I understand, Count… but still…

ZABRODSKY: [*Suddenly grasps that he's been talking to Sand*]. Ah!

[*Dryly*]. I am very sorry… All this is not to the point. It never occurred to me that I might… [*Cuts himself short*].

SAND: That you might lower yourself to talking to people like me about yourself?

ZABRODSKY: You have said it, sir. Yes.

DORA: [*Rises*]. Mr. Zabrodsky, we're not at all interested right now in your life history, in analyzing your intimate world. And we don't care what you feel toward us, whether you think talking to us is a degradation or not. We don't care whether or not you excuse yourself. We're not a court of justice. We only care about one thing: That this girl should begin living again the normal life of girls her age, that she should forget all the terrible things that have happened to her. You saved her life—but now she *knows*… and she's got to decide whether she'll choose a free, decent life, without fear and deceit or…—she'll decide. And that's the only reason we're still talking to you.

LENA: [*Is silent*].

ZABRODSKY: [*Who hasn't even glanced at Dora as she spoke*]. I know you have already made your decision, Lena. You always told me you would leave the day the war came to an end. Well, for you it has come to an end tonight.

LENA: [*Still silent*].

ZABRODSKY: Would you like me to beg your forgiveness? I will not. I shall beg pardon and forgiveness in another court. And as for you—I know very well: Either you will curse me for the rest of your life, and then—of what use is forgiveness!—or else you will curse *them*, after you see what they offer you there, in their free, beautiful world, in their decent, straightforward world, with their liberty—the liberty of strutting slaves. But now you must go to this world.

LENA: [*Still silent*].

SAND: We'll give you time to consider everything, Lena, and to decide for yourself.

DORA: Nobody can hold you here… [*Pause*].

LENA: I'm staying here. [*To* ZABRODSKY]. With you…

ZABRODSKY: [*Elated, but immediately rises and speaks as if treasuring a great pain*]. No. It is all over. It is finished. You will not remain here with me.

LENA: I want to stay.

DORA: Lena, listen…

ZABRODSKY: What will you do here now? Will you be the wife or mistress of the caretaker? Will you sell tickets to tourists who come here, to this *museum?* They—these two—have destroyed everything. It cannot be undone: you are not the lady of the castle because I am not its lord. This is the end.

LENA: Why are you torturing me? All of you! [*Makes a gesture of desperation*].

ZABRODSKY: Lena, understand, I want you to understand…

DORA: Mr. Zabrodsky, we all want her to understand…

SAND: Lena, you…

ZABRODSKY: Lena, I wanted to tell you…

SAND: Mr. Zabrodsky, wouldn't it be better to leave her alone just now and let her think and decide. After all, she's got to know what she's doing. Isn't that right, Lena?

LENA: [*Doesn't answer. It is obvious that she is engrossed in some private thoughts; she is undergoing a complex spiritual experience which none of the others can share*].

DORA: [*To* ZABRODSKY]. Why, when you say to her "Go," it's clear to her and to us too, that you're trying to hold on to her with all your might…

LENA: [*Suddenly*]. And with this telephone you can reach the city? [*Short Pause*].

ZABRODSKY: Yes…

LENA: You can talk with people?

ZABRODSKY: Yes…

LENA: You can talk to—let's say—the capital?

DORA: You want to call somebody up? Come…

LENA: No. [*Shrugs her shoulders*]. No. Why?

DORA: Then why did you ask? Maybe you want me to call up for you?

LENA: No. [*To* SAND]. I only wanted to know, if it's possible. Really…

[LENA *sinks back into her thoughts, as if she were not the crux of the conflict*].

ZABRODSKY: I did not want to hold you by force, Lena. I did not want to deceive you. But I deceived you.... I held you by force... I knew, that one day it would all be destroyed... but what there was, Lena... I wanted to guard for you—for us— this world which only the two of us knew... and then I...

DORA: Sir, why don't you let her think and decide! You're still all taken up with yourself! Even now you're not thinking about her...

ZABRODSKY: There was a world, Lena, in which the two of us, only the two of us lived...

LENA: [*As if coming out of a dream, yet still dreaming*]. And you used to open the windows?

ZABRODSKY: Which windows?

LENA: This window—here!

ZABRODSKY: This one?

LENA: Yes... here. This one!

ZABRODSKY: I—sometimes—during the day—yes...

LENA: And at night?

ZABRODSKY: No—at night I didn't open it—all these years...

LENA: But are you allowed to, are you allowed to open the window at night, are you?

ZABRODSKY: Yes.

LENA: [*Rises and advances to the window as if pulled by an unseen force. Draws the heavy curtain aside and looks outside. Then she turns out the lights. Moonlight*].

DORA & SAND: What are you doing?

LENA: [*Ignores them. Returns to the window and opens it wide. The room is inundated by moonlight. Lena raises herself up to the window sill. All move towards her, fearing she might throw herself out of the window. But she only leans out and utters a cry, as if calling someone in the garden or in the big forest. They look at her, amazed. Bathed in moonlight—she seems to be a vision. She settles herself on the sill and speaks to them and to herself*]. Such a moonlit night... there—the moon's outside.

And there's no war! You're allowed to shout, listen! [*Shouts again to the garden*]. How many years! How many years did I dream of being allowed to… please, come, you shout too, talk out loud! It's permitted now, there are no Nazis, nobody will come to kill us… [*For an instant, she looks at her hand in the moonlight, examines it, shakes the fingers*]. How lovely! No… maybe the dead have hands like these… [*Looks out again*]. This air! The garden is wet from the rain. Do you know what that is? It's the smell of the earth after rain! I haven't forgotten it… maybe it's the only thing I haven't forgotten… but that's it, now! It's a smell of… rotten leaves, yes! and mushrooms… the smell of mushrooms, yes! To run in the garden—barefoot… I always dreamt that this moment would come and I would open the window, and touch the leaves and the leaves and the branches, and the drops would fall on my head from the roof and wet my hair. Just like now. [*Smooths her hair with her hand and laughs*]. That's it. And there's the garden and… [*Sings a short tune to the night*]. Once in the spring, you remember, Count—do you remember?—I begged you so much—I so much wanted to smell the spring outside—I begged you—[*Suddenly to* DORA *and* SAND, *as if their presence was a matter of course*]. In my room, down there,—there's no window at all… I longed so much—for fresh air! I was very frightened… but I so much wanted to breathe this air! And you opened a small crack in the window, you put out the lights and opened a small crack. And from the garden came the smell of night—ah, I thought I would go mad! That was happiness… It was wonderful, Count, that you allowed me to open the window then… [*Suddenly jerked back to reality*]. But that was only a few months ago! The Nazis had gone by then, there was no… and if I had only known. I could have run in this garden… I could have opened the window then, talked out loud, shouted, shouted—like tonight… I could have done everything, anything… but—my God!— Four months! Two years! Two years and a half!—I want air, I want to run, to walk and walk… I want to,—my God! [*Pauses, listens*]. It's quiet. There are no birds in the garden—after the storm, ah, why it's night... [*She slips down from the window-sill. Passes them very quickly, very lightly. Goes over to the wall tapestry, presses something, and disappears behind the wall in silence. Only something like the creaking of a bolt is heard*].

ZABRODSKY: [*The first to understand what has happened, jumps to the secret door and beats on it with his fists*] Lena!

DORA & SAND: [*Screaming*]. Lena! Lena! [*No answer*].

DORA: Lena! [*No answer*]. She locked the door from the inside.

SAND: And can't you open it?

ZABRODSKY: [*Suddenly calm*]. No.

SAND: Don't you have a key?

ZABRODSKY: No.

SAND: I'm sure the door can be opened, I'm sure.

ZABRODSKY: No...

SAND: Go and bring the key, if you don't have it here; why she's got poison, she has poison hidden in the amulet...

ZABRODSKY: Poison? Yes...

SAND: Poison, I tell you, don't you understand?!

ZABRODSKY: Poison... I know... God will judge us...—

SAND: Maybe you'll stop thinking of yourself! Give me the key!

ZABRODSKY: I have no key, I've told you.

SAND: [*Gripping him powerfully*]. Give me the key, give it to me right now. [*Applying pressure*]. Right now, I tell you!

ZABRODSKY: [*Twisting in pain*]. I don't have one... it won't open. Let go!

SAND: [*Releases him*]. But she'll die... there, now she'll kill herself!

ZABRODSKY: The dead do not die twice, you have heard...

SAND: Nonsense! Who knows what she's doing there now!

ZABRODSKY: [*Sitting down in the armchair*]. Who?

SAND: Don't play the idiot. I tell you she's got poison, it's dangerous.

ZABRODSKY: Whom are you talking about?

SAND: [*To DORA*]. Look, now he's going mad...

ZABRODSKY: I am not mad, sir. I ask you, whom are you talking about?

SAND: About Lena, for God's sake!

ZABRODSKY: Who?

SAND: The girl who was just here, half a minute ago.

ZABRODSKY: [*Calmly*]. There was no one here besides the three of us.

DORA: [*The tension and fatigue have overcome her and now she begins to lose her sense of reality*]. How is that—there was no one?

ZABRODSKY: No one was here. It is a dream you dreamt, Madame. Or are still dreaming. Only we were in this room. You, Madame, Mr. Sand and myself. The three of us. No one else.

DORA: But I saw her, I talked to her, I touched her. She was here, just a moment ago. [*Stares at him blankly*]. I touched her…

ZABRODSKY: [*Laughs*]. When you dream—the dream is tangible. She was not here. No one was here. You dreamt.

SAND: But I didn't dream! [*Goes over to the wall tapestry; looks threateningly at Zabrodsky*].

ZABRODSKY: Go ahead!

SAND: [*Raises the tapestry, exposing a white, smooth wall, which reveals nothing. He runs his hand over it again and again. There is not the slightest sign of a secret door*]. Strange!

ZABRODSKY: Strange indeed. Very strange. You attack me. You speak of some key. You are both suffering from delusions. You can see for yourselves—no one was here. No one is here, it is inconceivable.

DORA: But… a moment ago that girl was here. Lena. She appeared when the clock struck. The clock with the cuckoo. She told us that she's been here in a secret room… for three years. She was… of course she was… here, the window's still open…

ZABRODSKY: Naturally. The moment I came in I saw you opening the window, Madame!

DORA: Me?

ZABRODSKY: [*To* SAND]. You saw how Madame went over to the window and opened it? And then she called out something into the garden.

DORA: Me?

SAND: I saw how Lena went over to the window and opened it, and shouted and sang and talked to the night. I saw it and heard it.

DORA: So did I.

ZABRODSKY: Yes, yes. This is a curious phenomenon. Two people sharing the same hallucination. It is strange indeed. When I rushed in here, after hearing Madame's scream, you were still talking about something. And then Mr. Sand attacked me and demanded some key... Perhaps the castle is really haunted by ghosts.

SAND: Don't expect me to believe such fairy-tales.

ZABRODSKY: You do not believe in such fairy-tales, sir, but that a girl can step out of a wall—which has no sign of a door—at the sound of a cuckoo—this you believe! That a girl can sit here captive for three years in peace time—this you believe! And you do not find it strange at all?

DORA: It's... Sand, what's going on here?

ZABRODSKY: Ah, what is going on here! Madame, I observed how tired you were tonight before we parted, and what a fright this castle gave you. You were over-wrought earlier in the evening, and I can well imagine how the misery you have seen in your work, the pain you have witnessed, the twisted lives of the children... yes, it is no simple matter—all this could easily give rise to delusions on a stormy night, in a house like this, which, moreover, has an owner who proclaims himself dead... perhaps my joke was not well taken, Madame, ...Please forgive me...

SAND: But I...

ZABRODSKY: And you, sir, have probably been certain until this very day that you see nothing but reality... May I remind you of what you told me earlier in the evening—you were wounded during the war—and you are not yet fully recovered—did you never see such fantasies when you were delirious with fever?

SAND: Please, Mr. Zabrodsky, this is not the time to discuss our psychology.

ZABRODSKY: But what shall I discuss when before me stand two people who see ghosts where none are to be found?... This is the source of your delusion—why, in our conversation at the tea table, we spoke of this, Madame. You asked me if the castle was haunted. And I said that it was. Then you informed me, Madame—for you are very brave—that you are not afraid of them...

DORA: Yes...

ZABRODSKY: [*Emphatically*]. So you see, all this was a dream. I am not too well versed in psychology, but I remember having read that sometimes two people share the very same delusion when subjected to the same stimuli—and not only two people—even much larger groups... the Hindus, for example, know very well how such things happen. But calm yourselves, after all I am here now.... I have dispelled the evil spirits... still, it is most interesting, how did it happen, actually?

DORA: [*Submitting completely*]. Sand wound the clock. The clock rang ten times. And then, Lena came out of the wall...

ZABRODSKY: Yes, that is exactly how you told it before. Out of the wall!

SAND: Not out of the wall. How you can twist words around. You know very well. She came out of a secret door which is under this tapestry.

ZABRODSKY: Secret doors exist only in novels for young ladies... There is no secret door there. You have seen for yourself.

SAND: But it was there.

ZABRODSKY: Would you like to check again? [*Rises, goes up to the tapestry, raises it*]. Well! [*No door can be seen.* SAND *feels the surface again*]. There you have it! Such things are found only in novels, in dreams. Lena was her name, you said?

DORA: Yes.

ZABRODSKY: [*Seats himself again in his place*]. Lena—a beautiful name. Yes... I also dreamt a dream. [*Unwittingly he falls into a reverie*]. Lena was her name. One day she came to me—and with her my youth came back... the old days had returned... the nights were—it was as if the moon rose here, in the castle… the prophecy had come true: There were neither living nor dead, neither young nor old… the truth was in memories become flesh… and if one of us were to die suddenly—that would be the gateway to another reality, a fiercer reality… for reality was a dream. We all dreamt.

SAND: [*Harshly*]. We'll find out right away! [*Turns on the light. In the electric glare, everything becomes more real. Sand goes over to the table*].

SAND: [*Very soberly*]. And now I'll tell you something, Count, this is where your real crime begins—beyond that secret door which can't be found… maybe we're already too late. But maybe—hand over the key right now!

ZABRODSKY: I have no key…

DORA: [*Now completely alert; Goes over to the telephone*].

ZABRODSKY: [*As DORA tries, unsuccessfully, to put her call through*]. And do you think there is anything more terrible than what you have done to me? Do you think you will frighten me with the Police? Do you think I wish her harm? She means a thousand times more to me than to you!

DORA: [*To the telephone*]. Hallo! Hallo! No answer, damn it! [*To ZABRODSKY*]. We'll see! Hallo!

ZABRODSKY: [*To SAND*]. The truth of the matter is, I have no key… what could I have done? It closes in such a way that only the person inside can open it…

SAND: Why didn't you say that right away?

ZABRODSKY: I said it but you didn't listen…

SAND: But she has poison…

ZABRODSKY: [*Doesn't answer. Sinks back into his own thoughts, mumbles*]. And he that overcometh shall not be hurt of the second death…

DORA: [*By the telephone*]. That won't help you! Hallo! Hallo!

[*At that very moment the secret door opens; as it opens slowly, it can be observed that part of the bookcase serves as a door. LENA comes out dressed in the clothes she wore the day she ran away from home. In this simple dress, she looks even more*]

Drama

childish than before, but the dreamlike quality is gone. She is, simply, a frightened young girl].

LENA: I changed my clothes... I couldn't have gone that way... [*To* DORA *&* SAND]. Will you take me with you?

DORA: [*Hands up*]. Well! [*Regaining her confident, professional manner*]. What sort of a question is that!

LENA: I can't stand it any more... I want—fresh air—outside.

DORA: Do you have any more belongings?

LENA: No. This is the way I came here.

DORA: [*To* SAND]. Do you have a blanket in the car? Now that the storm is over, we can go?

SAND: [*Silently looks at Zabrodsky, at Lena—it is obvious that he finds it difficult to adjust to this practical tone*]. Yes... we can... if we have enough...

DORA: We'll fill up at the nearest open gas station. [*To* LENA]. I'll just collect my things, in the room. [*To* SAND]. You... your books are already packed up downstairs... [*To* LENA]. We'll leave right away. I'll explain everything to you on the way. [*Goes to her room*].

LENA: [*Goes over to Sand. Stands by him as if seeking shelter and protection. Says apologetically*]. I opened the window... and then... I want to breathe fresh air outside...

SAND: You'll soon breathe fresh air, Lena. And now... Would you like me to step out for a moment?

LENA: [*In a fright*]. No, no!

ZABRODSKY: [*Looks at her*]. I won't stop you. [*To* SAND, *who makes a motion as if to leave*]. Please stay, sir! The two of us—she and I—have nothing more to say to each other. It is over for us! All dreams come to an end with the awakening. [LENA, *without looking at him, moves almost imperceptibly towards him*]. You need not give me your hand, I am not even sure I could feel it. You were—and you are no longer. I was and I no longer am.

LENA: [*Looks questioningly at Sand. He makes an encouraging gesture. To Zabrodsky, with great effort*]. Count...

ZABRODSKY: No. There is no need, Lena. You must go this way. You must forget everything if you wish to live there…in their world.

SAND: [*Takes Lena's hand*]. She'll live there.

ZABRODSKY: Evidently that is the only world which is now real. A reality of the wide-awake, the open-eyed. You have chosen it, and you must accept your choice. Dreams must be banished from the heart.

LENA: [*Again looks imploringly to Sand*].

SAND: Dreams that have ended—vanish of themselves…. But not all dreams end with the awakening. In the world of the wide-awake there are dreams—many dreams. Only they're dreamt differently… [*Sees her looking at the window*]. Yes—there, in the garden. There are trees. There are more gardens and trees. You know, maybe you still remember—you can lie under a tree—watching the sky through the branches… yes… and perhaps there's a wind… it doesn't matter. You're very tired. You lie stretched out, with your hands under your head… and daydream… open-eyed… the wide-awake dream in the light…

ZABRODSKY: So they think! They believe, in all honesty, that they really are dreaming! I am a great sinner, Lena, I have sinned against you—out of weakness. But I gave you a true dream! The dream was true—and if there was something false in it… who was the one who lied, Lena?

LENA: [*Holds the amulet lace around her throat*].

ZABRODSKY: Ah, you thought you were deceiving me? I knew. You carried your death with you always without telling me. But I knew… I said nothing, Lena, because each of us is entitled to a refuge from his fellow man…

SAND: But this refuge—was death!

ZABRODSKY: Death. Both of us—you and I, Lena, knew so much about death, that this bit of poison faded to insignificance in all the real death that surrounded us. This you learnt here. And now…

SAND: And now she'll learn something about life. Not everything—not all at once. In these years all of us learnt something about death. We learnt… yes… that death can sometimes be known in an instant. But to know life you must learn a great deal, little by little, not without difficulty—that takes all of a man's life, and only then—well, maybe he'll know something… but, [*smiles*], it's worthwhile.

ZABRODSKY: [*Looking at her, as if for the first time*]. Yes, Lena, all of life. You… you are… so young, Lena.

DORA: [*Enters dressed, with raincoat and briefcase*]. Well, then… we're ready. Let's go, Sand. Come, Lena. Goodbye, Mr. Zabrodsky.

SAND: [*Looks at Zabrodsky, wants to extend his hand. Hesitates.* ZABRODSKY *doesn't notice him.* SAND *bows slightly, shrugs his shoulders and goes*].

[ALL THREE *leave.* LENA *does not look back at what she is leaving behind. She clings to* SAND, *as if seeking protection from her past. They go out. After they leave,* ZABRODSKY *goes over to the window, lowers the curtains, puts out the side light, so that only the small lamp, which was on at the beginning of Act II, lights the room. He sits motionless in an armchair, as if he were one of the museum pieces. The cuckoo pops out and calls twelve times*].

ZABRODSKY: [*Raises his head slowly to the clock*]. Midnight.

Curtain

A Selected Bibliography of Books by Lea Goldberg*

Poetry:
Smoke Rings [Tabaot Ashan]. Iachdav, 1935.
The Green-Eyed Stalk [Shibolet Yerukat HaAyin]. Dfus Hanakda, 1940.
Songs in the Villages [Shir BaKefarim]. Dfus Hanakdan, 1942.
From My Old Home [MiBeiti HaYashan], 1942.
On the Flowering [Al HaPricha], 1948.
Samson's Love [Ahavat Shimshon]. Mikra Studio, 1952.
Lightning in the Morning [Barak BaBoker]. 1955.
Early and Late [Mukdam VeMeuchar], 1959.
With this Night [Im HaLaila HaZe], 1964.
A Collection of Poems [Yalkut Shirim]. Iachdav, 1970.
The Remains of Life [She'erit Hahayim], 1971.
Collected Poems [Shirim], 1986 (three volumes).

Plays:
The Lady of the Castle [Ba'alat HaArmon], 1956.

*Note: all the books were published by Sifriat Poalim, unless otherwise noted.

Plays [Mahazot], 1979.

Prose:
Letters from an Imaginary Journal [Michtavim MiNesiah Medumah].
    Davar, 1937.
And He is the Light [VeHu HaOr], 1946.
Encounter with a Poet [Pegisha Im Meshorer], 1952.
Letters and Diary [Michtavim veYoman]. Massada, 1978.
Collected Works [Ketavim], 1979.

This list does not include the numerous volumes of Goldberg's books for children, her books of translated literature or her literary criticism.

About the Translators

Rachel Tzvia Back—poet, translator and professor of literature—has lived in Israel since 1980 and in the Galilee since 2000. Her poetry and translations have appeared in numerous journals and anthologies, including *The Defiant Muse: Hebrew Feminist Poets from Antiquity to the Present*. She is the author of the critical work *Led by Language: the Poetry and Poetics of Susan Howe*, and of two poetry collections, *Azimuth* (Sheep Meadow Press 2001) and *The Buffalo Poems* (Duration Press 2003). Her Goldberg translations have recently been awarded a 2005 PEN Translation Fund Grant.

T. Carmi—poet, translator and editor—was born to a Hebrew-speaking family in New York City in 1925, and came to Israel in 1947, serving with the Israel Defence Forces for two years and then attending the Hebrew University. A past editor of *Ariel: The Israel Review of Arts and Letters*, he was visiting professor at Brandeis University, at Oxford, Stanford, and taught for many years at the Hebrew Union

College, Jerusalem. A favored participant at international poetry festivals, he was the recipient of many awards in Israel and abroad. He translated many plays into Hebrew, including Shakespeare's *A Midsummer Night's Dream*, *Othello*, *Measure for Measure* and *Hamlet*. Carmi's several collections of his own poetry in translation include *The Brass Serpent*, (1964), and *Somebody Like You* (1971), but he is perhaps best known outside the Hebrew-speaking world for *T.Carmi and Dan Pagis: Selected Poems*, translated by Stephen Mitchell, published in the Penguin Modern European Poets series (1976), and for the celebrated collection *The Penguin Book of Hebrew Verse*, (1981). He died in Jerusalem in 1994.

The fonts used in this book are from the Garamond family

The Toby Press publishes fine writing,
available at bookstores everywhere. For more information,
please contact *The* Toby Press at www.tobypress.com